Living Life As You Always Dreamed

A simple guide to the life you are born to live

Angelica Rose

Emails: angelheartofmotivation@gmail.com
Websites: https://angelroselove.wixsite.com/love

Cover Design, Zurigroup Steven Slamkowski 503-236-3377
steven@zurigroup.com

Published by JLR Publishing

ISBN 97809639304-1-5
Printed and bound in the United States of America
Library of Congress Catalog Card Number: 2002091524

Acknowledgment

I am eternally grateful to my connection to God and the Universe

Thank you Steven Slamkowski for doing such beautiful work on the cover

To friends and people who have touched my life in a profound and meaningful way

CONTENTS:

THE BEAUTY OF NATURE

The mountains are clear - The sky is blue
The flowers smell pretty and are wet from dew
Life flows like the ocean
The feelings of peace from releasing emotions, the joy will
increase- Angelica Rose

DIVINITY OF LOVE

M any have gone to churches, synagogues, retreat centers, monasteries, etc. as seekers to find purpose. While others have taken sacred vows to become nuns and monks to learn the secret. So what is the secret? Divine love is moving from the human self-absorbed focus, a form of selfish love, more fully into the genuine divine self, a strengthened inner being that resonates unconditional love. It is the letting go of the human self-absorbed ruling your life, which when in command, looks outside for what is already inside. When you allow the human self-absorbed focus part to run your life, it comes from separateness, a perspective of limitation, a place that pushes, tries to control, force and make things happen. The human self-absorbed focus desires to 'get' rather than share. This does not mean the human is bad. It actually is necessary to be able to live on this planet, as it is the human's job to protect you. Divine love is created when you go within and strengthen your connection to source-GOD-Universe, as a spirit being living a human life rather than a human striving to be spiritual.

Chapter 1
Believe In Yourself

Where is your focus on your path as you live life? Is it based on human self-absorbed running your life or GOD conscious choice? Living life from divine unconditional love, starts by turning within and strengthening the inner being. From that place, you share from a more nurturing place.

HAVING SELF-BELIEF

As one chooses to come from divine unconditional love, a spirit being living a human life, one will understand the strength of their inner being with greater self-belief. Strengthening the inner being is one step toward creating harmony between the body, mind and emotions and solidifying a connection to the inner spirit being. Then you move into greater respect for all living things on the planet. Strengthening the mind starts by quieting the mind chatter and from that place training it to have a more positive focus. One tool is to keep a daily gratitude journal, writing what you experienced each day that you're grateful for. It trains the mind to focus more on positives than the perceived negatives in life.

Having a healthy physical body entails eating healthy and exercising regularly. By eating healthy, you are feeding the body with nutrients and through exercise you are strengthening the body. Together they enhance vitality and well-being. To develop more inner love, you take steps toward nurturing and self-care. An exercise that supports that is to focus daily on things you appreciate and that make you feel happy. This will trigger your emotions toward inner joy which combined with nurturing and self-care builds self-worth. This chapter provides awareness and tools to further develop a higher self-belief. The development of our self-belief brings us to a higher level of fulfillment. When we take time to nurture our-self, we feel a greater love and self-respect. This helps us to feel more secure and fulfilled. The more secure we feel, the more we will enjoy living life. It's quite amazing when we lead our life with skill development, positive attitudes, and positive focus; We develop self-directed leadership and those around us feel inspired as well. We have more vitality in our activities. We feel inner joy and peace.

Feeling secure gives us the courage to take more risks in life. We believe in our talents, abilities and skills choosing to do new things and explore more. We feel a sense of freedom, an out of a box mentality, where we enjoy developing more of our skills and discovering latent talents. The relationships we have with others will also become healthier and more whole when we as individuals become healthier and more whole. Healthier relationships flourish as you learn to share from a genuine unconditional loving place, and have a readiness and openness to receiving. Having a healthy relationship starts with you. When you choose to walk the path of divine unconditional love, any unresolved issues will come up stemming from family upbringing, the environment you were brought up in and self-inflicted beliefs that don't serve your well-being. These unresolved issues are shown through experiences you encounter and in your relationships.

If you have any unresolved childhood issues, they could be projected in current situations and interactions with others. For instance, if you were brought up in a conditional loving environment or even an unloving environment, you may grow up with mistrust toward yourself and others. You may have a hard time taking proper care of yourself, since you blame yourself for the dysfunctional lifestyle you were raised in. You could have a hard time trusting your decisions in life fearing they will lead to disaster. You may end up relying on and expecting others to make your life decisions and bring you the joy, security, well-being, etc. that you want in life. You may have unrealistic expectations leaving you isolated from others, feeling lonely and victimized by the outcomes. You may personalize them, feeling it is your fault or blame another and become angry and bitter. This pattern leads to a vicious cycle of desiring to be loved, while simultaneously having a hard time opening up to it. You end up looking outside to others for the things you desire within, such as security, love, and joy. You may settle for relationships that require "fixing" due to low self-worth. Some of your relationships may consist of you caretaking and mediating others' problems.

You may feel you are required to please others, discounting and ignoring your own needs and desires. These relationships come from low self-worth and a lack of internal self-care. There's a longing for love and feelings of loneliness engulf you. Rather than fulfill your own needs of emotional love, joy, and security, you will look outside to others to try to meet them. Having a healthy loving relationship requires you to learn how to turn within for all your needs rather than looking outside for others to meet them. You realize that there is nothing wrong with meeting your needs emotionally and that is not being selfish. The greater the self-care, the healthier your self-image becomes and the more self-confident you feel. Eventually the longing you had for love will start to feel fulfilled and you will feel more connected in relationship to inner spirit and GOD-The Universe. The wisdom you acquire from your past experiences will help you open the parts of the heart that may have been shut down. The anger and pain experienced from the unjust, unfair and unloving behaviors will diminish and be replaced with deeper levels of love and inner peace.

When you choose to look at these experiences from a focus on having a peaceful outcome rather than from a victim mentality you're better able to understand what is being shown. Taking responsibility by looking at the gift behind the experiences and staying open to the lessons will help you accept and receive a greater understanding of the steps to take for peace and forgiveness. You will feel a deeper level of peace and start to embrace fully from your heart as you move forward in your life. As you develop a stronger inner strength based on love, you go out into the world with a desire to share rather than an expectation to receive. As you share from your heart joyously and unconditionally, you feel emotionally fulfilled and eventually receive back naturally. From that place you develop healthier relationships. Your relationships become more fulfilling and loving as a reflection of the love within. Choosing to have a positive attitude moves us away from the half-empty glass or perfectionism where we are not satisfied, to a full glass enjoying all. We enjoy more of who we are and appreciate what life brings us.

When you choose to appreciate the little things in life, you start to look at the beauty life has to offer. You are not as concerned with what others think or feel about you when it comes to their projections of insecurity. You have this freedom from self-absorption and live a more balanced life. Your perception of life is on beauty, joy, peace, love and gratitude. Have you ever walked into a room and seen a person who lights up the room with his or her energy? This person demonstrates exuberance-aliveness. He or she reflects an inner peace and joy, fully embracing and enjoying the moment and the experience. When we believe in our self and choose positive attitudes, we have a more positive focus on life. We put our attention on what we *Do* choose to experience rather than *Don't*. We come to understand that whatever we put our attention on long enough in our focus, thoughts and feelings we create in our experiences and in the level of success. It starts with how we feel inside. If we come from feelings of self-belief, our thoughts and feelings will be more positive. If we come from self-doubt, our thoughts and feelings will be more non-positive.

The greater our self-belief, the greater our success which includes financial security, enhancing our talents and abilities and achieving aspirations. Higher self-belief contributes to more positive thinking and joyful feelings. making it easier to stay focused on what we choose to experience. Having a peaceful and fulfilling relationship with yourself requires the ability to recognize and minimize your distracters, such as fear, self-doubt, negative thinking, worrying, etc. Having self-awareness and choosing to live a balanced lifestyle also means having the willingness, ability, and commitment to take steps to make it happen. If you experience self-doubt, it'll be easier to become distracted, thus affecting your well-being. Distracters hinder you from having whole healthy relationships, fulfillment and acquiring intentions. These distracters are powerless words, insecurities, limitations, negativity, fears, problem-focus, and time-wasters. They affect the way you view life and the way you live. What-ever you focus on long enough you start to create in your life. If you allow these distracters to dominate your focus, you'll perceive life from this place, experiencing more struggles and pain. Let's look further at how to improve the development the four areas— our self-belief, positive focus on what we choose to experience, improving skills, and positive attitude.

EMOTIONAL STRENGTH

High self-esteem is important for developing satisfying personal and business relationships as well as manifesting the life you desire. Your self-esteem fits along a continuum from non-positive to positive. Your level of self-esteem is a result of many combined factors such as your family upbringing, past relationships, and social environment. A low or non-positive self-image will not allow a person to reach their full potential and in most cases, is the root of many self-destructive habits. It is as if you are on this path toward your dream and it gets sabotaged each time you feel you are close to getting it. Subconsciously you could be sabotaging it due to an unworthiness belief, fears of success, or you trying to force it to happen.

On the other hand, you could be maturing so that you are ready for the fulfillment of this dream. This is where a high or positive image takes place. A high or positive self-image, allows you to lead a more productive and satisfying life. You have a strong internal belief that you are worthy of attaining only the highest good and you actually experience this in your daily life. You're committed to your intentions, staying focused and discerning accordingly. You are aware that all needs get met in time, have faith and believe. You experience your needs from an inner strength versus depending or expecting them from people. You act on things that will keep your heart open. You have a deep understanding that everything you need whether it is peace, joy or financial security, comes from **within** and it is experienced in your life according to your level of acceptance. As you strengthen your belief system, the greater you will feel the enrichment of your natural abundance and fulfillment in life.

LOWER TO HEALTHY SELF-ESTEEM

Becoming aware of the areas that can be improved upon is the first step in learning to increase your level of self-esteem. Awareness is 95% toward the process of transformation. Transformation is about refining and uncovering what is already inside of you and that is necessary to mature. It is not about changing, fixing, correcting anything or anyone because you and them are not broken. Having a belief about changing, fixing or correcting only contributes to lower self-esteem because your focus is on what is not good enough or working in your life and blaming results from that focus. As you become aware of unconscious and hidden beliefs that have been keeping you feeling stuck or stagnant and shifting them to healthier beliefs, the 'stagnant and stuck' parts of your life becomes free and your self-esteem improves. Your belief system also starts to become healthier and your outlook in life is positive, joyful and peaceful. The activities and friendships you make resonate from that healthier place as a mirror-reflection of all the amazing things you have done inwardly.

BELIEVE IN YOURSELF

Believe in yourself, for life is a journey.
It is not for one, it is for many.
There will be joy, there will be pain.
There will be loss, and there will be gain.
The trick is to laugh and have self belief.
For the wisdom you achieve, one may want to ask.
For life is a play, filled with many parts.
And if it comes from the heart, you have mastered your art.
- Angelica Rose

The following chart illustrates the differences between a higher self-esteem and a lower self-esteem. This will provide greater insight so you are able to release those dysfunctional areas and replace them with healthier one.

Compare the areas and see which ones you can improve on:

LOW SELF-ESTEEM	HEALTHY SELF-ESTEEM
Unworthy: Feeling low self worth which normally stems from a critical upbringing or experiences that you personalized as truth. You tend to take fewer risks in life and are fearful of failing.	*Worthy:* Feeling high self worth. Your inner being is strengthened so you have more confidence. You enjoy taking more risks in life and lead a more fulfilled lifestyle.
Dependent On Others: Depending on others to fulfill inner needs. No one can ever fulfill your inner needs. It can look as if the others can yet only you can truly fulfill your own needs since you know what those truly are.	*Self-Reliant:* Interdependent: Combining independent and dependent behaviors in a healthy and balanced way. Being whole and your own best friend, which entails self-love and self-care.
Self-Critical: Judging self, insecure, and playing a victim role feeling people are doing things "to you." Majority of the time, the behaviors are projections of what is going on inside of you.	*Self-Respect:* Honoring your values and beliefs from a higher truth. Transforming and Releasing the dysfunctional beliefs in a loving manner rather than through judgment.
Fix-Change-Correct Others: Attempting to change or make others to be more like the way you would like them to be. This comes from a place of insecurity.	*Acceptance of Others:* Allowing and accepting others and the way they choose to express their authenticity, talents & gifts from a more loving place.

Fear Driven: Giving your attention to your fears allowing them to run your life. You make your fears your enemy. Your perception is fear based and your reality is created from this place.	*Courage & Strength:* Fear is—False, Evidence, Appearing, Real. Fear is your friend. You have courage and strength to look at what fear is showing you to learn and grow and develop wisdom.
Struggle & Control: Not appreciating what you have and not choosing to live life fully, leads to unhappiness and boredom. Attempting to force outcomes beyond the appropriate timing as well as control situations and people so as to get what you want	*Trust (Allowing Timing):* Appreciating what you have, developing wisdom and living an adventurous lifestyle. Doing new things brings enjoyment and expansion within. You allow things to flow at the proper pace and trust in the universal timing.
Passive-Aggressive: Withhold expressing and then react the thoughts and emotions you're experiencing.	*Assertive:* Share feelings and thoughts with compassion and care.
Victimization: Feeling helpless, out of control and confused with unfavorable experiences. Making excuses for situations that felt unjust and unkind. Blaming yourself and/or others for your current experience.	*Making Choices and Taking Responsibility:* Improving experiences and situations you perceived as unfavorable from a growth perspective allows you to develop the wisdom to move forward in life.
Insecure: Deflated inner worth. Life situations are more difficult, causing struggles. Discounting self. Expect certain behaviors.	*Self-Confident:* Strong secure inner being. Building self-esteem through pampering and nurturing yourself.
Blaming the Past: Mind Chatter creating stories from past memories. Blaming the past for current life experiences.	*Living in the Moment:* Live in the present. Observe and transform the outdated beliefs so you can create a happier life.

Disharmony with the heart, body, and mind:	Harmony with the heart, body, and mind:
You don't feel happy and you choose to do nothing about it. You allow the mind to focus on non-positive thinking. You do not eat healthy or as healthy as you would like. You make excuses rather than exercise.	Throughout the day you monitor what you're feeling, choosing to have inner joy. You choose to focus on positive thinking. You eat healthy and exercise to have more vitality and well-being.
Deprivation Focus: Limited focus, believing there is not enough.	*Abundance Focus:* Unlimited potential. Know there is plenty.
Despair: Look to the outside for answers rather than going within. This can stem from past mistakes perceived as failures. As a result you feel unsure of what steps to take and fearful of repeating the same painful experiences, leading to feelings of despair and self-doubt	*Hope, Faith, Trust:* You go within for answers. Trusting that past mistakes helped you to learn and grow thereby preventing you from repeating the same mistakes. You take responsibility for your choices and actions, trusting your inner guidance, thereby making more effective decisions.
Love/Hate Relationships: Love/hate relationships are based on a part of you not accepting a part of yourself. You thereby attract the part you don't like.	*Unconditional Loving Relationships:* Sharing fully from the heart without expecting any return. Open to receiving, knowing you deserve it.
Paranoia & Mistrust: Feel mistrust and suspicious towards others' actions and their behaviors. Personalizing others' behaviors from a self-absorbed victim mentality. Feel you have to isolate and hide or protect yourself so *they* don't hurt you.	*Cautiousness & Self-Trust:* Trust your inner self for what is best in your current life situation. You stay open to suggestions others give and your inner guidance. When making decisions, you come from a place of self-love and trusting the universe.

Worry: Caught up in unhappiness, blaming, and playing victim.	*Concern:* Comfort emotions and choose to be happy.
Overly critical: Judging others. Labeling their beliefs as good, bad, right or wrong based on your beliefs. Righteous behavior.	*Accepting/Complimentary:* Nurturing and supportive. Accepting of others' beliefs, knowing you don't have to take them on as your own.
Powerless words: Constraint beliefs verbalized in your vocabulary projecting lack of self-belief.	*Power Words:* Confident beliefs verbalized in your vocabulary projecting high self-belief
Personalizing: Give your power away to others by allowing their critical words or unkind behaviors to affect you unfavorably. Self-absorbed where you focus more on what others are doing *to you.*	*Secure with Self:* Observe others' behavior subjectively. Question others' behavior for clarity. Reclaim self-love and inner peace by setting boundaries & taking a break from others' when necessary.
Unrealistic Expectations: Stems from your upbringing and belief systems. These expectations can come across as controlling & manipulative behaviors. Expectations lead to disappointment with the experience and/or the person you have them with.	*Anticipation:* More freedom to be authentic when you take responsibility for your life allowing others to take responsibility for their choices they make and their life. Choosing teamwork with behavior issues.
Failing mentality: Looks at every experience from the past. Bringing past experiences into the present choosing to believe it will repeat and you won't succeed. You tend to procrastinate or even quit.	*Miss-Take Mentality:* Look at the experience from the present. Knowing that this is a new opportunity to learn, grow and develop more skills from the experience. It is another chance to do it differently and improve on it.

Conditional: Give with an expectation of return puts a barrier on the receiving and the giving. It leads to expecting certain behaviors from others based on how each defines it. This causes relationship conflicts	*Unconditional:* Sharing from a place of whole complete love. Relationships learn, grow and mature in love and depth as you allow and accept. You are not looking for anything in return when you share.
Dependent/Independent: Independent behaves like they don't need anyone. Dependent behaves in a more needy. Both create isolation and a form of separation. The independent does many things by themselves. The dependent clings on to others more, at times pushing them away.	*Interdependent:* Go within first to fulfill inner needs- love, peace, security, and joy. Create emotional, mental, physical and spiritual harmony. Having interdependent relationships starts within, providing for whole, healthier, fulfilling interactions.
Murphy's Law: Belief that if anything is going to go wrong it will and it will won't be any fun. There is lots of blaming going on with yourself and possibly with others. Lots of insecurities and fears and complaining. Feeling helpless about what to do to improve it. Attempting to control some outcome	*Serendipity:* Belief that everything has a positive outcome. Chooses to accept each situation and the people involved for what it is and what it's not. Knows when to surrender to GOD-Universe and when to be pro-active in order to learn, grow & acquire wisdom from the lessons. Allows the outcome.
Problem Focus: Experience obstacles from a complaining mentality. You're Caught up in the emotions, blaming from a victim mentality. Find fault and taking little to no action to improve on the situation.	*Challenge Focus:* Experience obstacles from a solution-based mentality. Comforting emotions free of allowing them to run your life in a negative manner. Choosing to take action to improve on the situation.

Caretaker and Over-Please: Taking on other people's problems. Discount your own needs. Focus on correcting, fixing, or changing others	*Supportive:* Empathize, accept and offer suggestions., allowing other's to make their own decisions. A more playful attitude.
Self-Absorbed: Putting yourself ahead of others without considering the other person, their well-being or God causing more struggle.	*Self-Care:* Nurturing oneself and caring for all living things, including the environment as you contribute through recycling.

Outdated beliefs are beliefs that no longer serve your life. These outdated beliefs create conflicts and a separation from your inner spirit and God created by a human control. When you give your power to these outdated belief, they cause confusion from their separateness and disconnection, conflicts and struggle. The human ego goes into a fight, flight and protect mode. Thereby, they feed the 8 common distractions such as, self-doubt, problem-focus, negativity, powerless words, limitations, fears, judging, and time-wasters, causing confusion and pain. They create emotional weakness which comes in the form of prejudice, hate, abuse, disrespect, control, ignorance and judgment. They challenge your inner strength. When you're committed to peacefully and lovingly transforming them, they provide greater learning, growth and wisdom. This frees you from their chains that bind you, experiencing peace and joy.

Beliefs that are more in alignment with your spirit being, provide a deeper connection to GOD-The Universe. These beliefs create emotional strength, defined as genuine unconditional love, a form of divinity. Those who exemplify emotional strength demonstrate genuineness and inner fulfillment. There's a sense of inner peace, care, compassion and acceptance for all living things. This genuine peaceful expression is shown in their words, body language and their whole being. Life flows with greater ease and comfort, moving through lessons in a smoother fashion. You experience inner peace, joy, unconditional love, vitality, well-being and greater prosperity.

ONE WITH GOD

Being first *Doing* second
Connect to GOD as a Spirit Being having a human
experience
Sharing from the heart with joy
Wisdom expands the limited human mind to GREATNESS
-Angelica Rose

STEPS TO BUILDING SELF-ESTEEM

Everyone has the ability to transform their life, though some people wrongly assume they have no power to improve their level of self-esteem. The pain and misery, resulting from low self-esteem, can be minimized or avoided when you let go of the old dysfunctional behavioral styles, stop resisting and learn new functional behavioral styles. These new behavioral styles stem from your internal desires, values, beliefs and aspirations which can take time and tenacity on your part to develop, yet the rewards are many, such as personal growth, happiness and peace of mind.

Listed below are effective ways to build your self-esteem:

Take responsibility for your life.

Developing a confident and strong inner being supports a healthy process of being pro-active with your desired intentions.. Taking great self care of the body, mind and emotions and doing activities you enjoy in positive supportive environments open you up to experience a playful attitude thereby keeping you positive rather than taking things so serious. There use to be a time when people were rewarded for working long hours and not taking time out to relax. It is nice to see that more people are realizing the importance of living a balanced life as they take time out for recreation, themselves, their family, and the community in addition to work. Leading a balanced life provides enhanced feelings of joy and greater well-being. The alternative is caretaking others or discounting them all together, and not taking proper self-care which can eventually lead to resentment, hostility and physical ailments.

How do you behave in your relationships and in life situations? Do you come from a place of self-directed leadership, taking responsibility for your choices and actions? Or do you come from a place of blame and dependency, relying on others to motivate you, make decisions for you and accept the outcomes accordingly? Relying too heavily on others, leads to an unfilled life and stagnation and as a self-directed leader, you LIVE a life of adventure. Balancing your life, involving play and joy is important to avoid feeling unfulfilled, tired and bored with life. This can result in blame and low self-esteem.

Affirmations and pep talks:

Affirmations are an effective tool to improve our self-belief. They are positive words that we choose to shift our belief system in areas where we lack confidence, have a low self-image and self-worth. These positive words are put in the present tense as if you already have it and said daily. Using positive words is like being an actor or actress, where you are playing a different role in life, convincing yourself that you're better than you think you are. Your vocabulary shifts your attitude, which shifts your focus, which shifts your belief. This new vocabulary changes your thinking habits (programs) thereby changing your perceptions in life. With these new perceptions, you develop new behaviors and a different reality. One helpful technique with affirmations is to stand in front of the mirror and say them out loud. At first you may discount or not even hear what is being said, due to your mind used to hearing non-positive feedback in the area you are transforming. As you continually practice, the mind and emotions will eventually accept the new belief where you will hear it, see it, believe it and portray it in your life.

Affirmations and pep talks help to build your self-esteem and transform your attitude from non-positive to positive. As your attitude becomes positive, you are able to concentrate and stay focused on the positive outcomes rather the non-positive, avoiding conflicts, frustrations, anger and internal put-downs. When used properly, they can be very effective in reprogramming our beliefs and release old patterns and ways of looking at things. Let's say for example, you feel over-weight and dress in clothes that hide the parts of you that you dislike. You can write a statement that says-"I now accept my body." The first possible reaction may be, "yeah right" this is far from the truth. The more you dislike your body the more you'll treat it with hatred and disrespect. In order to lose the weight, it is important to accept and love the body as it is NOW. Then you can improve on the areas you feel necessary to help lose the weight. This way your focus is on what you wish to improve not what you hate. If you constantly verbalize say put-down statements, you can shift your mind programming to, "I am smart and I deserve the best."

After you write the affirmation, there are four steps to help you in shifting the belief system.

1) Look in the mirror each time you say the affirmation
2) Say the affirmation out loud with conviction and belief as if you believe it is true, thereby feeling it
3) Say the affirmation first thing in the morning, often through-out the day and right before you go to sleep
4) Reward yourself with hugs, loving compliments, pampering and small gifts to support you in feeling loved and cared for.

Psychologists discovered that it takes 3 weeks to break a pattern. Depending on how ingrained the pattern is it can take less than three weeks or more than 3 weeks. The important thing is to be patient and self-loving. At the beginning, you may experience challenges with your belief system, as you shift from an unhealthy self-image to a healthier one. You may experience inner feeling and thoughts attempting to get you to focus on the original belief. You may also experience people who might challenge you to hold on to your old belief rather than incorporate the new belief. The first few times you read the belief out loud, self-doubt and feelings of helplessness may arise. As you continue to stand strong with conviction and inner strength in this new belief you are incorporating in your life, eventually you'll start to literally hear the words and then feel them in your heart. Soon thereafter, you begin to believe the words and finally you will portray it and receive this new belief as a reflection from others.

Make situations and relationships comfortable for you. Don't adapt to uncomfortable ones.

Friends are people to enjoy life with, grow with, forgive and support. They're not ones you fix, change, judge, audition and criticize. I was working on this project and I remember this guy coming up to me from one of my classes and saying, "Would you help me to understand how to handle a situation?" "Sure I said what is it?" Then he began to share something that as a result of awareness and dedication, his life changed for the better. "I play basketball with this guy and every time I play, he finds things to judge me. It makes it difficult to enjoy playing the game with him." I said, "That could be pretty challenging feeling no matter what you do, you get judged." He agreed. I then asked him "have you ever judged anyone in your life recently." He first became defensive asking what that had to do with the situation. Then he answered yes. He realized that by him judging others, he was attracting what some spiritual people call Karma, a cause and effect situation. From that moment forward he agreed that he would be more aware of how he behaved with others. He chose to be kind and accepting of others. A few weeks later, he shared how the guy was being kinder toward him and more accepting. He was amazed how the transformation was affecting this other guy in addition to him feeling fulfillment in himself and with his friends.

It is important to accept others for who they are, not for who you want them to be. If the friendship is not a compatible friendship then parting may be the next step rather than think you can change them into someone you want them to be. Healthy relationships support each other's growth and learning curves rather than expecting them to bring you happiness, solve your problems, or fulfill your internal needs which lead to disappointment.

Make your own decisions rather than relying on others to make them for you.
Look to others for guidance in your fact-finding, weigh the best choices, trust your intuition and make the decisions accordingly. Realize that the mistakes you make are lessons to learn from so that you can avoid making the same mistakes. I remember how I listened more to my parents rather than my own guidance in my high school years when it came to choosing a major for college. They shared how great I was in math and how great I would be as an accountant. So I focused all my energy on being an accountant. I took subjects in this major and after the first year, I quickly discovered that I disliked accounting. I quickly changed the major from accounting to finance. I remember this one teacher who kept on telling me how I would be better off leaving college. He said I should find a husband and have children. While this other teacher who had similar beliefs made me work harder on assignments. In addition, he would make it very difficult for me to pass essay exams and at the same time I noticed how he made it very easy for a guy in the class. I decided to prove I could get an "A" in both classes so I spent majority of time on studying.

I received an 'A' in both classes by following all their guidelines and answering the questions exactly how they'd like them to be. When I graduated, I landed my first job with Warner Brothers International as their financial analyst. I remember walking down a street and seeing that guy working at a newsstand and hearing how he was unable to get a job in his field even though he had a high GPA. He got so discouraged after a few rejection letters and he finally gave up and settled for any job. I learned a valuable lesson from these two teachers- to *believe in myself and not quit.* After a few months of working at Warner Brothers International, out of curiosity I asked the boss why he hired me. He shared that it was due to my persistence and self-belief and how much I wanted the job by continuing to follow up even though I was told not to call and to wait. He said that it had nothing to do with experience since I had none— this was my first job out of college.

I look back now and realize how grateful I am that I went the business route, although more importantly I realize how important it was for me to follow my heart and believe in myself. By believing in yourself as you persist in attaining your desires, you will feel motivated and inspired with life. Some goals change or become less important in attaining them as you become wiser.

Respect others' opinions.

A difference of opinion is good. There is a difference in having an opinion and being disagreeable with others. The latter is quite annoying and pushes people away. A student in one of the classes I taught walked in late and yelled out in the middle of my conversation, "I don't agree." I looked at her amused by her comment and was curious, so I asked what she didn't agree with. She began to share her feelings and beliefs. Even though I didn't agree with them, I still chose to respect them. I shared how people have differences of opinions and how we can learn from them. She again began in a loud voice to disagree, so I replied that I accept her having an opinion and I respect it. In addition I respect my own opinion even though we might disagree. She continued to disagree. I discovered that no matter what I would share from that moment forward, she would attempt to argue and disagree. So I said, "so be it," and continued my teaching.

I believe having different opinions is what makes us the unique individuals as long as it doesn't affect others' well-being. Being open-minded to others 'opinions doesn't necessarily mean doing what others believe. Thru listening, you could pick pertinent information to help shift old paradigms that no longer are suitable in your life. Or it could simply mean two differences of opinion. When someone disagrees, you can say "good, we have a difference of an opinion; maybe I can learn something from you, please explain why you disagree." As you listen to their response, you could pick up new information to apply and learn new things, building your base of knowledge and self-esteem. You notice from this approach, you are being more subjective rather than personalizing their differences of opinion and letting it affect your self-worth.

Share unconditionally.

If you give with an expectation of return, the majority of the time you will be disappointed when those expectations are not met. This disappointment can lead to bitterness, anger and mistrust resulting in insecurities and low self-esteem. Majority of the time when people give conditionally they want attention in some area of their life. It's as if they're giving from a place of wanting something similar to the way they gave.

Have you ever experienced a person giving you a gift whether it is tangible or non-tangible and then feeling judged when you didn't give back in the form of a gift or even a thank you? Although a simple thank you is considered a kind gesture, this is a form of conditional giving. There is an expectation tied to the giving.

In your process of unconditional sharing, it is important to learn discernment and create balance. For example, certain people have a continual habit of taking and not returning at all. These people come from a self-absorbed place and have insecurities. Others have a continual habit of giving and not being open to receiving. This unbalance leads to resentment from others and manipulative behaviors. If you are a giving person and surround yourself with takers, then you will eventually feel deprived and expect in return. If you are a taking person, you'll behave in ways that are manipulative in getting what you want from others.

As you become more balanced with sharing, you will come to a more fulfilled, whole place. During this process of balancing, those who had a tendency to give too much may go through a self-absorption phase in their life, as they are moving through some lessons in life around nurturing themselves. Those people who become aware of the self-absorbed selfish behaviors and choose to change by giving will come to understand the true meaning of unconditional sharing. When you share unconditionally, people will feel more comfortable being around you and will want to share unconditionally with you. They won't feel that you are giving with this high level of expectation or demand for something in return. In time, you will feel more joyful in your sharing as well as learn to receive.

Respect yourself.

Being your own best friend, a great tool to self-respect, consists of self-love, pampering, complimenting, and being kind when you make mistakes. It is throwing the word *perfectionism* out of your vocabulary, realizing that you are here on this planet to learn and grow. Therefore you are aware that making mistakes is part of the learning process. When we were first learning to walk, we didn't fall and think of that as failing or not being good enough. We didn't focus on being perfect at walking. We stayed in the moment and focused on getting up and walking. We were determined to get on our feet and move to the other side of the room for mom's or dad's hug, for a toy, or whatever else we were determined to get our little hands on. Our focus was on achieving the result not on being perfect at it. So as adults, we have the opportunity to acquire our heart's desires and to live a life we always dreamed by taking the time to focus on our desired outcome with belief and conviction and to be proactive with universal timing. We can live a more fulfilled life as we learn to stay in the moment and enjoy what we have, transform any dysfunctional beliefs to uncover our inner strength and connect to GOD-The Universe as a spirit being rather than a human controlled being.

TRUE LEADERSHIP

If I lead will I become the person I choose to be? If I lead will
I stay in truth and integrity or end up wanting to flee? If I
lead will I be accepted for who I am and what I believe or
will I experience what seems like rejection? If I lead will I be
appreciated for who I am and what I see, the experience of
the 'light' I choose to be? The answer I discovered is within
me by learning to be forever free

-Angelica Rose

SELF-DIRECTED LEADERSHIP

Leadership is defined in many ways. True effective self-
leadership is comprised of four common areas.

- Self-belief, a belief in who you are as a person and
  demonstrating loving self care.
- Positive focus, where you choose to keep your attention
  in the moment and on gratitude.
- Positive attitude where you choose to enjoy life and be
  open to what it offers rather than just live life.
- Skill Development, where you enhance the skills
  necessary to bring best in you.

If any of the four is out of balance, the result will be an
imbalance in the way you operate as a self-directed leader in
life. In addition, you will start to experience unfulfilled
feelings and 'stuckness' in certain areas of your life.

TRUE LEADERSHIP

What is your definition of leadership? Please take a moment
to write it down. Now write your definition of self-directed
leadership. After you have done this, look at the words *self-
directed* leadership? Is it in a form of an action – *doing*
something before *being* something? Before you can take
some form of action, it is imperative to *BE* an effective self-
directed leader. Having a fulfilling lifestyle starts with <u>being</u>
connected to source-GOD first and listen. Otherwise you

follow some outdated belief and repeating the same pattern in your life. Clarity and direction starts to become clear and from that place, pro-action is apparent. Without listening for guidance you could act from a fear driven place resulting it outcomes that you don't want.

In going forward with your vision, as you take some form of action based on your moment of clarity, insight and direction, you could experience obstacles .Depending on how you perceive these obstacles and how attached you get to the outcome, your life will either flow naturally or you will experience chaos and frustrations. If you perceive obstacles in the form of *problems*, you are coming from a Murphy's Law Syndrome which says that if something can go wrong it will occur at the worst possible time. Below is the domino effect of this focus.

Murphy's Law Syndrome:

ξ

Obstacles perceived as problems

ξ

Focus is on the 8 common distractions-problems, fears, negativity, self-doubt, limitations, judging, powerless words and time-wasters

ξ

Blame self and – or others

ξ

Attract a pattern of more problems

ξ

Force or Control outcome

ξ

Impatience with the timing

ξ

Experience unpleasant feelings and thoughts

ξ

Wallow in self-pity and worry

ξ

Result in procrastination and/or quitting

ξ

Experience feeling helpless and out of control

If you continue to focus on the problems you will eventually experience frustration and chaos. If your focus is on the problems due to fears, self-doubts, or any form of limitation, such as time, resources and/or lack, you will eventually start to experience a pattern of attracting more problems coupled with unpleasant feelings and thoughts. On the other hand, as you experience obstacles, if you perceive them as *challenges*, you are coming from a Serendipity focus. From a Serendipity process, your focus will be on finding solutions, embracing your feelings, the 'we' mentality and success will be enhanced. Comparatively, Murphy Law Syndrome focuses on complaining and a 'me' mentality. Below is the domino effect of this focus:

Serendipity Focus:

ξ

Obstacles perceived as challenges

ξ

Focus is on the *8 Enhancers* - challenges, appreciation, positive attitudes, self-belief, unlimited potential, acceptance-discernment, power words and freedom of controlling time

ξ

Acceptance

ξ

Allow universal timing - staying present in the moment

ξ

Experience pleasant feelings and thoughts

ξ

Experience and comfort concerns

ξ

Be pro-active

ξ

Enhanced success

ξ

Experience fulfillment

With a Serendipity Focus, you have unlimited potential and start looking for the resources and what can work productively. You have a real strong belief in the mission at hand and become pro-active. People enter your life who can be supportive. At times you may perceive the faced obstacles as problems, focusing on Murphy's Law Syndrome, being unconsciously incompetent in some area of life. Then you become consciously aware of this incompetency either through others or from within. This doesn't mean you're incompetent as a person. Rather there is something in your life that is preventing you from moving forward in a free flowing manner. Without the awareness we go through a pattern of repeating the same 'mistakes' until we learn and acquire wisdom from the lesson.

As we face obstacles in front of us from a Serendipitous place, we go through a process of acceptance for what the obstacle is and what it is not, embrace it, surrender to GOD-Universe and allow clarity to unfold naturally. With acceptance comes greater understanding from a place of trust and faith. Alternatively coming from Murphy Law Syndrome, we go through a process of attempting to understand what the obstacle is, then our beliefs kick in either causing more friction from a dysfunctional belief or greater maturing from a belief that is functional yet requires more learning. If we resist the lesson, judge it, force some form of outcome, we create more struggle and unnecessary pain.

Both Murphy Law and Serendipity will get us through the obstacle. Murphy Law takes an exorbitant amount of time, struggle and the 8 distractions discussed in Chapter 4. Serendipity puts us in a place of experiencing more inner joy, peace, wisdom and love in a more easeful, flowing manner. Awareness is ninety-five percent towards solving it. Through acceptance we cone to greater understanding. Through a desire to understand, we come from our beliefs which could lead to struggle, if they are not serving us or if the belief is in conflict with another. If we choose to shift to a more positive outlook, we will learn from these mistakes in a more pleasurable manner than that of

Murphy Law. Through continual practice with a positive focus, we eventually become skilled and enhance success and fulfillment where we no longer require practice. This is called, The Cycle of Development of which I will share more about in chapter 4.

When we're solving obstacles from a problem mentality, we'll experience a perception of lack of time and less joy in life. This is because there's an emotional attachment to the outcome, trying to control or make it happen and playing victim to our circumstances with a tendency of doing nothing to solve the problem. We end up taking an exhausting amount of time trying to create a future desire in the present when the timing may not be right. We focus on what we don't have creating more problems. And as a result, we'll become emotionally drained from worry or physically exhausted from overdoing. When we are solving challenges in life if we take the Serendipity approach, we'll experience a flow with time and more joy in life. This is because we let go of the attachment to the problem and the 'me' struggle mentality and focus on the solution and a 'we' mentality.

We step back from when we want the solution to happen and allow it to happen in its own time, called 'Universal Timing. For many people this could be a very difficult step to accept. We stay in faith and trust. Finally we focus on appreciating what we do have rather than what we don't. From this place, we are living life more fully and consciously present in the moment. As a result, we will accept and enjoy life more. When using the Serendipity approach in making effective decisions, our whole focus and perception shifts from fear to inner guidance. With the Murphy's Law Syndrome approach in decision-making, choices will be fear based and from insecurity. The choices that are made from a fear-based place, lead to one problem after another. This will lead to feelings of anxiety and self-doubt. I will give you an example for clarification. Please write down a desire that you would like to achieve in your life and then list all the benefits that you would gain from attaining it. Listing the benefits is a self-motivating tool to keep you moving forward when facing obstacles. Through the process of attaining the desire, you can incur an obstacle. The first decision is now about to be made based on how you look at this obstacle. As you look at this obstacle, do you perceive it as a problem- a failing mentality or as a challenge-an opportunity to grow, learn, become wiser? Which focus do you choose?

If you look at the obstacle from a problem-perception mentality, you will be faced with one or more common distractions. These distractions will start initially with your perception of looking at the obstacle as a problem, which has a limited perspective and outdated belief systems. As you make your first decision from this place, your focus is on what you don't want. You start coming more from a victim place, a blaming of self or of others. If you continue down this path, you will be facing additional distractions in a variety of ways. These distractions can come in one or any combination such as **judging, limitations, fears, negativity, problems, self-doubt, powerless words, and time-wasters**. The longer you choose to stay on this road, the more you play the victim role, accusing situations and others for the decisions you made or of those who made them for you. Since *your focus now is on what you don't want,* you will continue to attract more problems and end up in self-doubt and insecurity. Your decisions are coming from struggle and a 'me' focus, from a limited perception based on what you currently know.

Eventually not knowing what to do, you may procrastinate, quit or continue to repeat this vicious cycle in misery and self-induced pain. The attachment you have to the outcome only creates more intensity. The results of holding on to figuring things out, controlling or making things happen creates emotional distraught. It is quite an eye opener to discover the more you hold on to something, the longer it takes to get it and the more struggles you face; whether it be trying to understand situations, controlling outcomes, or trying to make the future become the present. Approaching each challenge from a Serendipity approach, immediately moves you out of the drama mentality to that of a peaceful solution 'we' mentality. The 'we' comes from your connection to source-GOD first as a spirit being living a human life. To acquire insights from a higher unlimited knowing and greater wisdom through acceptance and learning.

From the awareness that you are spirit being having a human experience, you know that you are not your feelings, thoughts or body you *experience them*. Therefore you can look at the challenge with an open mind, and unlimited perspective staying open to solutions. With challenges comes learning, and you are aware that from the lesson comes growth and wisdom making you a wiser person. You accept the challenge for what it is and what it is not and appreciate what the challenge is showing you. You choose to be present in the moment with a positive attitude, staying open for the clarity and insights. Once you receive the clarity and insights, you take proactive steps to create favorable results. With any obstacles you incur, you have a great opportunity to attract supportive people who will provide insights to help you learn the lessons with regard to the challenge you are facing. You experience faith and trust with regard to the challenge. Your self-esteem is further enhanced feeling calmer, peaceful, and excited. You become motivated, learn the lesson at hand and eventually move forward to the next phase in your adventurous life. This is what expansive learning is all about.

From this place of learning, you become a self-directed leader ready and willing to expand your comfort zone with new lessons and opportunities to experience greater awareness, insights and wisdom. You become a role model to those who are facing similar life lessons and challenges. People will talk favorably about you. You could become one of the chosen ones that have these gifts that support others to an awakened awareness that they are spirit beings leading a human life. Living as a spirit being having a human experience and connected to GOD-The Universe is oneness living. When you attempt to control a desire outcome from people or situations, you experience a disconnection from GOD. That is duality living.

OPEN YOUR HEART

As you open your heart to new beginnings and allow, the old
melts away. The old is nothing but a yesterday that no
longer fits in to the new today.
Fear is only - *False, Evidence, Appearing, Real.*
Fear is a friend, showing you what no longer is true.
The greatness of what you have become can no longer fit in
to what has been, and even greater is yet to come.
As you open your heart to joy and play, the struggle no
longer can be. As you open your heart to enjoying the
moment, the mind chatter has no place to be.
-Angelica Rose

MOTIVATION THROUGH POSITIVE FOCUS

If we continue to focus feelings and thoughts on what
we don't want we will eventually get just that- *what we don't
want.* The more we stay in our truth of enlightenment, in
addition to the desires we wish in life, the easier it will be to
feel joy within and more fulfilled in our lifestyle. Our truth
of enlightenment entails connecting to GOD-The Universe
as a spirit being living in the moment and listening with a
silent mind and open heart for clarity and direction.
Strengthening the inner being, supports the process of
releasing outdated beliefs, providing a greater awareness of
our spirit being. Through goal attainment we go through
lessons helping us to grow and acquire wisdom to strengthen
the inner being. As a self-directed leader, you can look at 4
components to strengthen, self-belief, positive focus, a
positive attitude and skill enhancement.

If we're to be proactive with our aspirations as a self-
directed leader from a Serendipity Focus, our outlook on life
and outcome is more favorable. When using the Serendipity
approach in making effective decisions, our whole focus and
perception shifts from fear to inner guidance. In the process
of attaining aspirations, any obstacles we incur, is perceived
as a solution based opportunity. Our decision now is made
from the perspective of positive focused feelings, thoughts

and beliefs such as **appreciation, positive attitudes, self-belief, unlimited potential, acceptance-discernment, power words and freedom from controlling time.** If we continue down this road, our decisions and the responsibility for our decisions come more from a place of acceptance, appreciation, allowing universal timing and staying present or fully conscious in the moment. When faced with additional obstacles, we look more for inner guidance and to experts for additional support and education. We experience more pleasant feelings and thoughts through our pro-active steps and receive more favorable outcomes.

By surrendering all forms of control, staying in acceptance & allowing insights to naturally flow you will be guided more easily to the proper events, situations and people. It is important to understand that guidance comes from your spirit being connected to GOD-The Universe rather than attempting to get answers from the human mind, which is limited and use to familiar patterns. Patience for this guidance can be very challenging and yet it creates more peace, faith and trust when allowed. Through allowing universal timing and guidance, there will be an easier flow with life and thereby creating more favorable outcomes. The more you focus on what you *choose to experience* and *let it go, allow the timing to be right,* the *quicker* it materializes, if it is for the highest good and if it is part of the grand plan of what you are here for.

Living life with vitality, harmony, peace, joy and greater unconditional love is acquired through both the awareness of striving for goals and strengthening the inner being as a spirit being living a human life connected to GOD-The Universe. Some call this Enlightenment. The greater the Enlightenment the less the focus is on human desires. The miracles become apparent in your life which provides even greater more expansive experiences than that of the human desires.

Serendipity Focus:

ξ

Obstacles perceived as challenges

ξ

Focus is on *8 Enhancers* - challenges, appreciation, positive attitudes, self-belief, unlimited potential, acceptance-discernment, power words and freedom of controlling time

ξ

Acceptance

ξ

Allow universal timing- staying present in the moment

ξ

Experience pleasant feelings and thoughts

ξ

Experience concerns and comfort

ξ

Be pro-active

ξ

Enhanced success

ξ

Experience fulfillment

Shifting our attention from any of the 8 distractions that impact our life and putting the attention more on the 8 enhancers are key tools in having a positive focus, joyfulness and a better attitude. Also, staying away from "fixing-correcting-entertaining" negative situations and experiences in the conversations we have with others and moving more into acceptance of what is and what is not. It is healthy to walk away from downers, accepting where they are at their levels of growth, blessing them rather than judging. To experience greater peace, joy and love start with self-love and unconditional love of others. To keep a positive focus and to choose positive thoughts, and develop self-belief; this frees the mind from bias thinking and judgment and preventing you from experiencing what you judging. If you experience negative people, keep your focus on the positive rather than on the drama. This will assist in shifting their focus from the drama to a more positive perspective and keep you from leaving feeling drained.

Staying present in your day-to-day experiences and taking proper self-care prevents you from getting caught up in someone else's drama. If you start to get caught up in another's drama, you can reclaim your personal power by calming the mind chatter, embracing the feelings to calm them down, relaxing the body and reconnecting to GOD-The Universe. Sometimes you have to walk away from the drama to do this. Stay *loving in the heart, keep attention on the positive rather than the drama, and stay clear of trying to fix, judge or correct others.* Developing a relaxation tool box helps to strengthen your inner being so that stressful situations and drama oriented people have less negative impact on you. This tool box consists of making a list of nurturing self-care and pro-active activities to create harmony, vitality and well-being in the body, mind and emotions. Through daily practice, you create a habit which becomes a source to easily use under ALL situations. Your list can start with eating healthy, exercising, practicing yoga to relax the body and meditating.

Meditating is a tool to help quiet the mind chatter, calm emotions and free attention from the don't wants to what you choose to experience. It supports positive focus, where you can choose positive thinking and joyful feelings. By shifting thoughts and feelings toward the positive, you start to find things to appreciate and feel greater inner love. Self-care and nurture helps build higher self-esteem. If you practice one minute or more a day focusing on appreciation through imagery or on a tangible object, you create feelings of greater inner love and joy. Another tool is proper breathing. This immediately will calm the emotions, quiet the mind and relax the body. Put one hand on the stomach and another on the heart and notice where your breath is. Now take a breath in through the nose hold it and then let it out through the mouth. To deepen the intake of your breath, you can take a breath, hold it and then another through the nose before exhaling out of the mouth. Go slowly. If you get light headed, slow down and take normal breathes. After 3-5 times of this type of breathing, you will notice a relaxation, calmness and more peace in the mind, emotions and body.

By developing a relaxation tool box and consistently practicing it on a daily basis, you minimize stress in your life and maybe even eliminate it all together. Your days become more relaxed and with any challenge you are more equipped to shift easily into the relaxation tool box. You are aware on how to immediately calm the emotions, quiet the mind chatter and relax the body. From there, you are able to make choices that support you rather than fear based choices that create more problems and struggles. Upon strengthening the connection with your inner spirit being and GOD-The Universe, you start to resonate pure love and gratefulness and you connect with others from a similar place. As you do this, you will come to realize it is not necessary to protect yourself from taking in other's energy. The feeling of taking in others' energy is about not staying centered in one's own truth and belief systems. Taking in a lower form of energy and feeling drained is about interacting from a place of separation from GOD and from not having a strengthened inner being.

THE DIFFERENCE BETWEEN CONCERN & WORRY

There is a difference between concern with challenges and worry with problems.

A person who worries dwells on their problems and complains, moans, and groans. Yet does nothing about them.

A person who chooses to focus on obstacles as challenges knows they are lessons to learn, opportunities for growth, and wisdom to achieve and share. They take action to resolve them without worry or too much care

The attitude is not of `Murphy's Law, where one believes bad things happen like a victim
The attitude is `Serendipity`, where one believes positive outcomes are behind the doors leading to wisdom
- Angelica Rose

DISTRACTIONS

Distractions limit or hold you back from getting where you would like to go, whether it is to accomplish goals or feeling more fulfilled in your life.

There are 8 common distractions

Fears	Non-positive Attitude
Judging	Powerless Words
Self-Doubts	Limitations
Problem Focus	Time-wasters

The mind is like a computer. What you feed it is processed and out creates that reality in your life. In other words, whatever you focus on expands in your life. If you focus on lack, deprivation, anger, mistrust, fear, and unworthiness, you will attract situations and people that reflect that focus. Your behaviors will also reflect what you focus on in your belief system. The pain is there in addition to the drama, struggles and frustrations. The good news is that this can be transformed. The length of time it takes is based on your commitment and willingness to transform the distracters to enhancers. Sometimes beliefs can tangled up with the distractions. Some beliefs can be core beliefs tangled up with a web of beliefs. It is like peeling an onion until you get to the core belief that is dysfunctional and transforming it with love. It takes inner strength, trust, faith and courage to persist in the removal of old patterns and habits.

Letting go of human control, surrendering, listening and allowing GOD-Universal guidance, makes it easier to process through any potential obstacles. Surrendering is where you give up the desire to control the outcome, force the results, and overwork to make something happen. In place you have a deep knowing, acceptance and eventually a greater understanding from an intuitive level on what action to take. You flow with life, enjoying the moment, embracing each experience, and make connections with people. So how does one detect, transform the dysfunctional beliefs and let go of control? The process of removing the outdated beliefs is like peeling an onion. Looking at the beliefs that no longer serve your well-being, with the analogy of the onion. The outer layers of the onion represent the less matured parts based on beliefs that don't serve you that turned into dysfunctional behavior patterns and transforming them into healthier behavior patterns. This is the path of divinity. Walking the path of divinity takes commitment, courage, trust, faith, persistence and strengthening the inner being. It is the process of examining the unconscious parts of yourself, and through genuine unconditional love transforming them, becoming more evolved and mature. As the outdated beliefs are peeled away through transformation, wisdom and enlightenment is developed. As you go within, connect and listen to GOD, or whatever word you use to connect to source, you'll be guided on what steps to take to help you remove the barriers.

Meditation is one of the tools discussed in building your relaxation tool box. It's a wonderful tool to help quiet the mind and calm the emotions so you can hear the inner voice of wisdom. It is the ability to focus on relaxing and tuning in while in meditation, rather than being concerned with the length of time one meditates, that is important. For some, learning to relax and tuning in takes shorter amounts of time than others. Centering within, is a process of learning how to relax the body, quiet the mind and open the heart. There are many tools used in meditation to help relax and tune in such as music, candles, chanting, focusing on breathing, visualization using colors or putting your focus and attention on the heart. It can be fun to experiment with a variety or use just one tool to help you relax and center yourself, so that you can tune in, connect to GOD, and listen for any guidance that may arise.

CYCLE OF DEVELOPMENT

The CYCLE OF DEVELOPMENT is another tool used to strengthen one's inner being. It is also used in the process of developing skills. The Cycle of development is a great tool to detect and transform any of the 8 common distractions into enhancers as well as attain goals.

CYCLE OF DEVELOPMENT

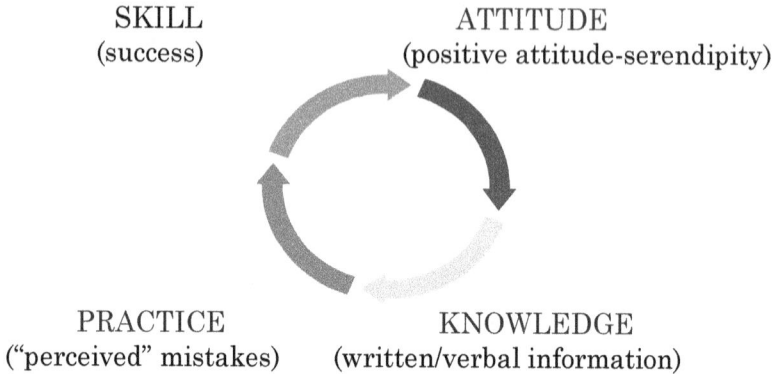

SKILL	ATTITUDE
(success)	(positive attitude-serendipity)

PRACTICE	KNOWLEDGE
("perceived" mistakes)	(written/verbal information)

In the Cycle of Development, attitude is the starting point. Keeping a positive attitude will help you move through life learning and growing more easily with each lesson. There are two ways we can approach attitude, one is an open-minded approach called Serendipity. The other is a closed-minded approach called Murphy's Law Syndrome. Serendipity, being the more open-minded approach teaches us from a positive perspective. Murphy's Law, being a more close-minded approach, teaches us from a non-positive perspective. With Murphy's Law Syndrome, our focus is on problems, blaming, moaning and groaning taking little to no proactive steps. We become lazy and experience struggles, resulting in procrastination, and even quitting. Murphy's Law Focus leads to experiencing feelings of frustration, insecurity, drama, helplessness, victimization, and negative thinking, putting us in a place where we don't know what to do. Ever been there? It is a pretty lonely place, unless you find another Murphy Law focused person-Misery loves company. That is a lose lost situation.

The great news is we can choose the Serendipity Focus. Some may start in the Murphy's Law Syndrome, yet we don't have to continue there. Awareness is 95% of getting clarity, focus and direction to solving challenges. Through a decision of shifting our focus the minute we start to feel unpleasant feelings and/or have non-positive thoughts to more positive thoughts, joyful feelings and taking proactive steps, we can move from Murphy's Law Syndrome to Serendipity. The next step after Attitude, in the Cycle of Development, is Knowledge which comes in two forms- written and verbal. You gather the information and do one of 2 things with it. You can either focus your attention on any of the 8 common distractions feeling somewhat stuck in the process of learning.

Secondly you can choose to stay positive in your focus and apply what you learned through Practice, the next step in the Cycle of Development, to become more skilled. At times, through education, some of the information you receive just clicks and not much practice is necessary. Other areas require more practice rather than sitting on this knowledge and taking no further action. Sitting on knowledge will provide something though, an educated butt, yet this isn't what leads your life, even though some may think so. Applying Serendipity in the practice stage of the Cycle of Development, we get passed the laziness mentality and solidify what you are learning.

With Murphy Law Syndrome in the practice stage, any of the 8 common distractions will attempt to grab your attention, internally through belief systems and externally through others trying to dominate your attention. The internal includes stuff such as fears, insecurities, non-positive talk, deprivation focus, time-wasters, self-doubt, etc. The external includes distractions, such as judgment, negativity, time wasters, learning lessons perceived as problems, and criticism. Those distractions can be perceived through your belief systems in two ways. One way to perceive these distractions is through believing one is failing. Through this process we continue a repeated pattern of learning lessons until we get the lesson. Depending on how you handle these distractions, you will either continue forward or get stuck and feel held back. When we perceive experiences as failures, we go into Murphy's Law Syndrome and we feel stuck, unable to move forward.

Alternatively we can choose to shift our focus from distractions, such as fears, negativity, doubt, judgment, etc to a more positive focus. The more proactive approach is through Serendipity, where we initially perceive these distractions as mistakes. Eventually with the Serendipity focus, we come to understand, learn and attain more wisdom. Through this process we are better able to move forward into new experiences in our life. Mistakes help you learn, grow and become wiser. With wisdom, you prevent the tendency of repeating the same mistake. You learn that challenges are disguised as opportunities to help you move forward toward attaining your desired goal, make more money or further develop your talents or any combination of the three. The sooner you move from a failure mentality to one of learning through mistakes, the quicker you get out of feeling stuck, lost, or confused and move toward more success. When we become aware of our failure perception, we can shift our perception to understand that we are merely making mistakes or 'miss-takes' in our experiences.

Learning the Cycle of Development will help you remember Serendipity Focus with more ease especially under stressful situations. Your life will feel more fulfilling and you will experience life situations more efficiently because you won't feel as stuck or lost. In addition, by understanding the Cycle of Development, if you start to feel stuck or lost, you will become aware of it sooner and know how to get unstuck and receive clarity on what to do next. Reviewing the differences between a Murphy Law Syndrome focus and a Serendipity Focus. With Murphy's Law, everything is a *problem*. In Serendipity everything is a *challenge*. There is a difference — problems don't feel good and challenges motivate you. With Murphy's Law, there is blaming from focusing on the problems. With Serendipity Focus, you become aware of the challenges embrace your feelings, and choose to find solutions. Now Feel the difference between Murphy Law and Serendipity versus just thinking about the difference. Rather than sympathizing, attached to the emotions, moaning and groaning, as experienced in Murphy's Law, you allow and embrace the situation and your feelings, surrender to GOD, accept what is and what is not, and know everything is going to be OK.

When you experience empathy, you embrace the emotions becoming less emotionally attached. This helps you move into a positive thinking and focus, giving you clarity and direction on what steps to take to help you find the answers. When you clear on what steps to take, and become proactive with them, you get closer toward attaining your success rather than procrastinating or quitting. Success can mean money, achieving goals or simply feeling more fulfilled within. Many have a prime motivator initially, whether it starts with goals, money or how you utilize your talents to experience more fulfilled. Each of these three can end up interchanging with the other two. When we apply our talents more fully, are clear on our goals and handle money wisely, we lead a more balanced lifestyle. If you're not utilizing your talents to the fullest or lack self-belief with how you express yourself, you miss out on living life to its fullest. Experiencing new things or trying something new is a way to break the mundane parts of your life and become more adventurous and fulfilled in life.

When you feel fulfilled, you experience inner peace, joy and motivation. Each time you achieve a new level of growth, your comfort zone expands and you start to feel more confident and comfortable taking on more risks. As a result, you don't allow the distractions such as, limitations, fears, and negativity or lack focus to dominate your life. Your success is created from a desire that you choose to attain. Having clarity and focus on the desire, commitment and becoming proactive leads you toward fruition. Without focus or clarity you are walking around with a blindfold on wondering what it is you desire in life and how to begin creating it. Staying focused on what you choose to experience in life rather than the distractions is a self-motivating tool to start and complete the tasks at hand. Whatever you focus on long enough you create from that reality. If you focus on your distractions, you start to move in the direction that will back up those beliefs, thereby creating what you don't want. When you choose to have a positive focus, you create a reality that mirrors those beliefs. Having a vision, feeling it in your heart and high self-belief are powerful tools for manifestation. Before you take any form of action, it is important to strengthen the inner *"being."* Self-directed leaders stay open to developing new skills. Remember to make sure that the desired goal is for the highest good of all concerned and that it is part of the grand plan of why you are here.

CAR DEMONSTRATION

ATTITUDE: Think about when you first learned how to drive a car. Go back two days before you drove a car and now you don't know how to drive a car. Remember your reasons you wanted to drive a car, the desires you had? You may have thought of some of the benefits of getting a driver's license, such as to get out of the house, to have more freedom, to show your friends you could drive or to get a date. Many different reasons motivated you learn to drive a car. Maybe you had to convince your parents to teach you how to drive. So you said, "I want to learn how to drive a car," knowing the benefits associated with the driver's license. You saw in the mind what it would be like if you had that permit, had the keys in your hand, that freedom. Your *attitude* was positive, "I can do it!"

KNOWLEDGE: You got the book of rules and regulations and some of you skimmed through it, learning the basics such as, *what are the posted signs and what are the speed limit regulations?* The remainder of you memorized each word to make sure you passed the test. Remember?

PRACTICE: When it came to taking the test some of you passed the first time and others had to retake it making you study more intently. During this time, some of you may have focused on any of the 8 commons distractions, such as fears, insecurities and self-doubt. Upon retaking the test, maybe you procrastinated or quit for a short period of time.

SKILL: When you saw how some of your friends passed, you remembered the benefits of passing both the written and road test and you were inspired again, so you retook the written test and passed.

AN EXAMPLE OF ALL 4 STAGES IN THE CYCLE OF DEVELOPMENT:

The next step was the preparation for the driving portion to get the driver's license. You took the time to learn the rules and regulations behind the wheel, practicing driving the car. Your parent(s), sibling(s), or the motor vehicle instructor started praying for their life, showing great courage. You got behind the wheel, face forward, seat belt on, hands shaking a little, keys in the ignition, doors locked and if you had a clutch on top of all this to learn-wow! Remember this? You turned the key in the ignition, possibly too much hearing a screeching sound, turned the wheel too much, and/or hit the gas and then braked too hard. Some of you may have made wide turns, hit a garbage can or curb and hopefully nothing else along the way.

By now the other person in the car was probably more scared than you. You smile to ease both your concerns and theirs. You either stayed in a Serendipity Focus remembering that you are practicing and making mistakes or shifted into Murphy's Law and felt like a failure. The latter, made you feel stuck in your distractions, resulting in procrastination or quitting for some period of time. Thoughts like, "I am not going to pass this test, I can't park the car" all these self-doubts and fears went through your mind. In remembering the benefits, you received comfort, realizing this is part of an experience to help you learn. You made the decision to keep practicing and got behind the wheel. You started to remember to ease up, relax and calm down not turning the wheel too much, or hitting the gas and break as hard. With enough practice you got better, and eventually developed the skill of driving. Now you drive with one hand on the wheel, water bottle in the hand, cell phone, talking to friends, etc. You became confident and passed the driving test giving you a new success in life.

It is the same thing in life, whether it's a tangible thing like driving a car or intangible, it all comes from within. Only you can make the necessary changes that keep you in a Serendipity focus. With continual practice, patience and kindness with oneself the process gets easier. It is like anything else you are attempting to learn in life. It starts with a positive open-minded attitude and desire, learning the steps how to do it, commitment to practicing with patience and trust and eventually the skill is developed. When we learn self-directed leadership and combine it with effective communication, we then are better able to have more effective relationships with others. Self-directed is again first connecting to GOD through your inner spirit being rather than the human limited belief system. By being an effective unconditionally loving self-directed leader, you are better prepared to have healthier relationships with others. As we learn to develop our self-esteem and self-belief, we then are better able to solidify our inner strength.

VISUALIZATION FOR MANIFESTATION

Visualization is a technique to help you move more in the direction of what you choose rather than what you don't want. Visualization is used heavily in sports. In fact it was proven with two teams of basketball players both teams had the same amount of time. One team visualized a positive outcome of getting the baskets in the hoop without practicing. The other team practiced shooting free throws. When they were brought together to shoot free throws the team that visualized without practicing got more balls in the basket than those that actually practiced. Why? Because they believed they could do it and they didn't allow any distractions, such as fears, self- doubt, or insecurities to hold them back. Visualization is a more effective tool to helping you get where you choose to go because you see and feel it prior to doing it. Whereas if you go out into the world only with the framework of 'doing' then there is a greater tendency to get caught up in confusion, failing, self-blame, procrastination and quitting.

Through "doing" only, what happens is the focus in on what is going wrong and any of the 8 common personal distractions come into play. Common fears such as fear of failing, rejection, unknown and success may arise. You begin to experience not being good enough, fearful to moving into areas you have not been in before and personalizing others' unpleasant behaviors. You may start to experience judging where you are labeling good, bad, right and wrong in the experience. You start to perceive the obstacles as problems and you emotionally blame and find fault. The problems build as you look at the situation with negativity and have a focus on what you don't want. You experience lots of self-doubt and insecurities. You create limitations and it eventually leads to many time- wasters, preventing you from getting effective outcomes.

You can be your own best friend or your biggest enemy and hold yourself back from happiness. Having a failing mentality is where the focus is on what is going wrong rather than you seeing and feeling your own success within. The more you focus on these internal distractions, the more you will make the same pattern of mistakes over and over and over again. As a result of this continual focus, you start to behave in ways that demonstrate Murphy's Law Syndrome-where you focus on obstacles as problems. This perception leads you to react with negativity and blame without taking any proactive steps to resolve the challenge.

Visualization allows for clarity of what it is you are striving for. It helps to reduce confusion and enhances concentration and focus. Visualization starts with self-conviction where you see, feel, and believe in what you are choosing to experience in the desired outcome as if you already have it. This combined with self-belief, the outcome being for the highest good of all concerned, it's part of your grand plan and allowing the proper universal timing, will help you attain effective proactive steps to manifestation. As you apply visualization as one of your key tools, it motivates you when you are going into unknown areas of your life. It assists in providing clarity, focus and direction with the unknown. This will support you on staying on the Serendipity focus path, leading you toward greater accomplishments and more fulfillment in life. You will go further in that unknown territory than you would if you go out there and just 'wing it. What will end up happening through visualization is that you will experience some of your own internal distractions and you become aware of them. With regard to solving challenges in life, awareness is 95% of the solution and the 5% is the commitment to transforming the dysfunctional beliefs. As you become aware of those internal distractions and decide to examine them, you begin to understand what the pattern is that is keeping you stuck or holding you back.

As discussed in an earlier chapter, Serendipity is defined as opportunities for growth and wisdom as you take proactive steps toward resolution or attainment. As we face obstacles, we perceive them as challenges rather than as problems. Our emotions are coming from a place of concern rather than worrying. Worrying comes more from an emotional and mental non-positive attachment as well as a focus on things going wrong. Concern, comes more from a place of faith and trust that things will be OK and all will be taken care of. As a result of focusing on faith and trust, one is better able to take action to move forward with more confidence and self-belief. As we move away from emotional and mental attachment and focus more on solutions, we are moving into pro-action. When we embrace the moment and our feelings, we become more relaxed in each moment. As a result, our attitudes are more focused on the positives and on enjoying the process. Through the process we achieve wisdom and our success is enhanced. This takes less time, rather than wasting an exorbitant amount of time or feeling stressed out by the perception of lack of time. We have learned to flow with time and trust Universal timing. We experience inner peace, joy, faith and trust.

Here is an exercise for you to do that will start the process in helping you attain more effective outcomes in your life. Visualize a goal or experience you would like to receive in your life. If you start to feel or hear self-talk on any of the distractions discussed, make a list. Then make a list of steps to take to help you attain the goal. Release any biased thoughts or judgments, as they can hold you back. In fact, act like you are an inventor coming up with ideas never shown before. Now sit quietly and connect to GOD and listen for the next step. Each day stay aware of any messages. It could come in hunches, in reading something, through others, etc. Allow the clarity, the proper timing and sources to show up on its own timing. If clarity doesn't come, start with the best step that feels appropriate to take. Have fun.

If any distractions arise, add them to the list you started. As you take the necessary steps to attain this goal and are faced with additional distractions, add those to your list. Categorize the list into major areas such as fear, self-doubt, insecurities, etc. Use the suggestions listed in the next chapter to help you minimize these distractions. Watch how much easier it is for you to attain the desired goal now that the distractions are no longer dominating your focus and life and that you have strengthened your inner being and connection to GOD.

FEAR - YOUR ENEMY OR FRIEND?

Fear - One gives so much power to
Fear - Resisting and it follows
Fear - Trying to ignore as it continues to pour
Fear - Fighting it as it stays in your mind with might
"Fear" - One cries! as clearing one's eyes
"Fear" - A friend? A question to bear
Fear - Become aware
Fear - A friend for enlightenment to share
Fear - Wisdom, upon one's knowing
Fear - No longer an enemy, for courage is showing
-Angelica Rose

LEARNING TO LET GO OF THE
DISTRACTIONS AND LIVING LIFE FULLY

Acceptance, Faith, Trust, Believing vs. Fears:

There are four common fears: *fear of failing, fear of rejection, fear of the unknown* and *fear of success.* When you perceive your obstacles from a failing mentality, your focus is on what is wrong, labeling yourself and others as bad or incompetent. You'll have a tendency to get caught up in unworthy thoughts and emotions. Eventually this focus will lead to feeling stuck, blocking you from taking action and moving forward. This type of focus will lead you on the path of attracting more non-positive and unfulfilling experiences. If you continue focusing your thoughts and feelings in a non-positive way, the outcomes may eventually lead to procrastination or quitting all together.

A healthy approach to obstacles is to perceive them as challenges to overcome rather than problems from a victim mentality. Perceiving obstacles as challenges helps you have a positive focus and receive opportunities for growth and advancement. Continuing in this direction, you will be more open to new opportunities, overcome any obstacles with more ease and develop more wisdom from any mistakes you make, thus avoiding repeating the same pattern. A student in a class I taught looked at mistakes as a 'miss-take,' another chance to do it again improving on it. Shifting our perception to allowing for mistakes and moving away from a failing mentality gives us a better understanding of all experiences. When we come to a full understanding of this, we are less likely to be so hard on ourselves and thus we are better equipped to let go of perfectionism.

As we look at understanding *fear* as a whole, fear is an illusion appearing real. Fear standing for, *False Evidence Appearing Real.* What is so amazing about fear is that it is very convincing. It will do whatever it takes to catch your attention, entice you and make you believe in it. The great gift of fear is it is really our friend not our enemy. It helps us learn and understand where our blocks with regard to unconscious dysfunctional beliefs that are dominating our life experiences. When we learn to focus our attention on positives and embrace the lesson rather than resist, hate, or try to push it away, we will move forward in a more enlightened manner. The lesson will teach us and thereby we can move on rather than continually repeat the lesson in a different manner over again. I have seen people get so caught up in the illusion of outdated beliefs that they buy a "room in this hotel of illusion" and become frustrated, moan and groan, and do nothing about it. Continuing on with the story day after day, the hotel becomes an illusionary 'house' they own. While others have personally learned to take a proactive approach and look for resolution, surrendering the emotions and thoughts, thereby permanently moving out of the 'room in this hotel of illusion.'

Faith and trust is more powerful and provides the genuine truth than the illusion that is currently being seen. Any drama causes unpleasant outcomes and misery while appreciating all in life is about celebration and joy. As you choose to release the attachments to the fears, surrender the attachment of wanting to know, and to let go of the attention on the *False Evidence Appearing Real* you come to eventually understand the lesson behind it more quickly. Remember some lessons you may not understand until months or even years later. Learn the importance of letting go of trying to figure things out and instead accept, embrace and enjoy the moment more.

Fear of failing:

I recommend eliminating the word 'failing' from your vocabulary and eventually you'll behave as if it doesn't exist. One student in a class I taught said, "I enjoy taking your class so much and I am afraid I will fail." I noticed how she had so much fear of not doing well and her attention was so focused on failing that it affected her emotionally and mentally. She had difficulty sleeping, concentrating and her thoughts were constantly on her not being good enough. I educated her on how it would be healthier if she let go of being so hard on herself and give up believing in something that may never happen. I explained that she is better than she believes and pointed out how quickly she picked up the information that was being taught and how she would share it and then immediately discount the responses. She was amazed by this information and thanked me. After 5 weeks of attending the class, I noticed how she became more relaxed and confident. As you let go of fear of failing, you begin to allow for learning and growing. You realize life is about learning rather than behaving as if you have to be perfect at everything you get involved in.

When you are striving for a goal, you go through a process of learning lessons and releasing any obstacles that are in the way of attaining your desired goal. During this process it is important to take it one day at a time and to stay in the moment. Acknowledging your daily accomplishments, helps you stay positive and in the faith that you will achieve the goal. You can set a target date and understand certain factors are necessary in attaining the goal such as, meeting people who are important for this goal, your own growing and learning, and appropriate universal timing rather than your own timing. Questioning and observing experienced people will assist you in the attainment of your goal in a more effective manner and provide educational information along the way.

- **Take it one step at a time (the process)**
- **Stay in the present moment**
- **Allow for what seems like *mistakes*; they are learning lessons to excel *not failures***
- **Acknowledge daily accomplishments**
- **Forgive yourself if you miss time deadlines**
- **Question and Observe experienced people in the area of interest**
- **Use visualization to create positive results**
- **Believe in self and what you choose to attain**

Fear of rejection:

If you experience fear of rejection, you look at the rejection as a form of personalization thus affecting how you feel about yourself. You give your power away to another or to the experience you fear, you allow the situation or person to judge you and put a value on your character, personality, or the manner in which you are behaving. If you take it to heart then you could give so much power to it that it becomes your reality. You behave in ways that confirm this belief system. You begin to demonstrate to others that they know more about you than you do. Eventually, it affects your self-esteem and your self-worth is then based on how others feel about you. To personalize every unpleasant facial expression, mannerism and behavior personally in any encounter only decreases your self-worth.

Putting your attention on self-care and self-love is one step toward moving away from perceiving other's behavior as a form of 'rejection.' A healthy way to examine the situation is to take the 'you' out of the situation and to use observation and discernment. When you are able to take the personalization 'you' out from the so called rejection, then you can look at the situation from a more subjective place, rather than a participatory place, and get a better understanding of the lesson behind the situation. Through observation and questioning, you will discover whether the person is projecting their own insecurities onto you in the form of blame or judgment or if it is indeed an area in which you can improve.

The majority of the time it had nothing to do with you rather a personal experiences they had with another, not feeling well or bad days they were having. If the criticism is about you, you can look at it subjectively. Behind the perceived rejection is a critique, information for you to learn from. It is the manner in which it is delivered that comes across as a criticism where the personalization comes into play. In questioning others, you realize that the rejection is not a personal thing, rather a lesson to help learn, grow and become wiser. By listening and focusing more on *what* the person is saying rather than *how* he or she is saying it, you are more equipped to accept and learn rather than personalize and feel rejected. 'Rejection' is either a reflection, projection or an opportunity to learn a lesson and become wiser. The choice is to get beyond the emotions, learn and grow from the experience, so you avoid repeating the same lesson.

- **Question the area of 'concern/rejection' with the individual**
- **Observe the situation subjectively to help you grow rather than as a criticism**
- **Say affirmations on the insecure area**
- **Detach and deep breath to relax & avoid getting too serious**
- **Listen to *what* they are saying vs. *how* they're saying it to avoid personalization**

Fear of unknown:

On average, 20% of the population will look at the area of the unknown territory in a positive way and discover new ways to create or enjoy life. They are moving into this unknown territory to expand their comfort zone, realizing few have been here where they have chosen to be. They look at it as opportunities where many skills are developed. Self-directed leaders understand that they don't have to go alone and that having a narrow focus and thinking their way is the only way can cause more challenges, frustrations and obstacles then if they remain open minded to others' suggestions. They search out experienced people and education to acquire more knowledge in the process of exploring unknown territory. They have the opportunity to discern what information the experts are sharing that will support them in the area they are seeking more knowledge.

Self-directed leaders know that through the experiences of educated people and through educating themselves, they are expanding their comfort zone and reducing their fear of the unknown. They understand that being in unknown territory is an opportunity for growth, wisdom and advancement. They're able to use intuition, self-belief and education from experts to acquire the knowledge to get wherever it is they want to go more efficiently.

- **Talk to others who are supportive, positive and trustworthy**
- **Inquire education from experts in the area you are learning**
- **Stay positive, focused and patient**
- **Take it 1 day at a time**
- **Have trust in self & GOD that everything will be taken care**

Fear of success:

Fear of success is the opposite of failing and yet some fear it as much as failing. Some people are so use to going through hardship and struggle that they have this expectation that in order to succeed it has to be difficult or that they are not worthy of success. It is as if they are so use to hardship that they don't allow success to come in an easier way. If someone is not ready for success or feels unworthy of it, the person can unconsciously or consciously self-sabotage their own success. Those that are ready for success may feel uncomfortable in regard to possibly losing their friends or family due to outgrowing those that choose not to succeed in their own endeavors. Are you willing to let go of something that could hold you back from complete enjoyment in life? There is a saying, 'misery loves company.' As you choose to enjoy life, grow and improve your life, you will meet others with the same focus. If friends aren't supportive and caring of themselves or you, it may be healthier to let them go. Initially it may feel lonely until you reach your new plateau, eventually you will find new friends that encourage rather than discourage.

Success in any endeavor, whether it be financial, emotional well being, spiritual enlightenment, or physical vitality, is a process. The process includes high self-esteem and pro-action with the desire, willingness and commitment to move on to greater experiences. Dreams are attained with greater ease as you observe and release any obstacles you face, find experts to help you with areas you may feel stuck in or to acquire more information, strengthen the inner being to prepare you for the next phase, meet the appropriate people and take action based on universal timing.

As we let go of the problem-oriented mentality, we start to let go of the emotional and mental attachments and release the fear driven focus. The attachments we have can hold us back from attaining desired outcomes. These attachments, if we look at them closely, stem from a fear of some kind- *False Evidence Appearing so Real.* Fear comes from an illusion that we chose to believe so deeply that it becomes our reality demonstrated through our beliefs. This fear driven focus, if we give it power and don't transmute what the fear is sharing, leads us toward procrastination, and possibly quitting. We are trained to *DO* when it comes to attaining outcomes, rather than *planning* what we are choosing to attain first prior to the doing. And during the process of attaining the goal, many of us continue to overdo rather than *observe what the obstacles are showing us.* As a result, we end up working harder rather than smarter. We focus on our insecurities and failing. We end up doing *TOO* much and exhausting our self along the way. When we learn to stop and examine what is motivating us, fears or divinity, we will have a better understanding on how to proceed.

Releasing our focus on being fear driven starts with learning to understand the difference between human control- the 'me' mentality and divinity- GOD and inner being strength. Human control pushes to overdo and divinity allows, it simply lets go of that which is not of our highest good. Divinity comes from inner peace, unconditional love, joy and a more serendipity focus with any obstacles we face toward the desired goals and experiences we face in life. Thus, we avoid repeating the lessons over again. With a Serendipity focus, we are ready to move into a solution based focus where we embrace and appreciate each moment throughout the day. Our attention is on appreciation, a self-motivating tool that keeps us pumped and positive. This is a great way to lead a life of joy and adventure rather than merely live life.

As we compare the human ego control with the higher conscious spirit being, human ego control comes from a lack of maturity and evolvement. The higher conscious spirit being is connected to GOD-The Universe sharing unconditional love and coming from compassion and an understanding of oneness with all. Human ego control is very powerful and can be convincing if you allow it. It can push you into any of the 8 common distractions:

Fears	Non-positive Attitude
Judging	Powerless Words
Self-Doubts	Limitations
Problem Focus	Time-wasters

Recognizing your biggest distraction and how it affects you is a big step in moving from human ego control to that of divine trust and faith. I believe in making ego your friend vs. your enemy since it is part of you. The only difference is not allowing it to control your life by disciplining the thoughts, loving yourself and giving service to others. Society has trained us to overdo and ignore listening to our own inner guidance, to attach to things that are superficial in nature for more success, beauty, etc. no matter what it takes. As a result some people have forgotten what I consider to be the true meaning of us being here: *To learn to love unconditionally, accept one another and come from compassion and peace.* You have free will with the choices you make in life. You can discipline your thoughts to that of gratitude, unlimited focus and positive thinking; love yourself more and embrace the parts of yourself that require nurturing, and appreciate all things. When we look at fear as a friend to teach, rather than resist or hate it, we come to accept and receive greater understanding of what steps to take and what it's teaching us. Fear teaches us what to let go of and the lesson behind the fear. Some are so use to letting the fears motivate us to react and over do. When what is necessary is to simply listen, relax and trust more.

Attachments hold us back from freedom. These attachments are merely chains that bind us. Letting go of these attachments frees the 'chains' that bind us, allowing for freedom to live life more fully. Fear comes from a place of anxiousness, forcing and controlling. Divinity comes from a peaceful place, an intuitive place and a place of comfort. Surrendering the areas in your life where you have no control in the timing of attainment, helps to allow proper flowing. Controlling or forcing rather than allowing and going with the flow, is not going to speed up the attainment. It slows it down. The more you hold on to something that you desire to come into fruition, the longer it takes to get it. It is like watching a pot of water boil. The minute you let go of trying to force the desired goal to materialize, any 'stuckness' in your life is released and you start to move like a boat gliding on a river, smoothly and with ease. The stronger the hold you have, the greater the attachment, the more challenges you face. The more you let go and allow, the freer and the more secure you feel, making it easier to attain the desired goal. Have you ever heard the statement,

"I always seem to get what I don't want and it takes forever to get what I do want?" Notice the 'wants' in the vocabulary. They come from a belief system of not having and possibly an underline unconscious belief of not deserving it. The harder the challenge, the greater the tendency is to want to quit. Learning, growing, readiness for the new and universal timing plays a huge role in the manifestations of life dreams. Allowing is important, as well as knowing when to *be* and when to *do*. That BEING comes prior to the DOING. The meaning of 'Being' is to be your true authentic self and from that place you tune in and listen for guidance so you come to understand what is necessary at the current moment. You have trust and faith that guidance comes in its own time. 'Doing' means to be proactive with the guidance you receive and using inner being strength to do the best in the situation based on what you currently know to do. Moving from a fear driven focus to one of divinity entails learning to listen to the inner voice. A red flag to knowing you are letting the ego control is when the body feels anxious, the mind confused and the emotions reactive.

In BEING one with your TRUE divine authentic self, the body feels centered, the mind is peaceful and the emotions respond from love. Eventually you will just BE in the moment in complete acceptance, peace, love and joy free of analyzing. Balance is the operative word between knowing when to just *be* and when to *act* on guidance. Walking a spiritual path takes courage, tenacity, patience and love. Moving from the place of human control living to a spirit being living a human life. Initially as a human living a spiritual life, you have some out dated beliefs that require transformation and some healthy belief systems. Some of the out dated beliefs are hidden in the unconscious mind and others apparent through awareness. As you transform them to healthier beliefs, you start to uncover your truth of your spirit. You become aware and experience yourself as a spirit being living a human life. From this place expansiveness occurs, a stronger connection to GOD that is so amazing. You experience mysticism and oneness with all living things and you appreciate it all. You have this deep desire to share from a pure loving place. Through enlightenment more people will come to recognize that peace comes from accepting one another and a willingness to work together, to embrace each other rather than fight, and to learn to embrace the parts within that are not as mature. If we *nurture*, rather than hate the parts we are evolving within, we will have more peace with our self.

CONTROL OR JUST BE

As one let's go of control and decides to just be, the moment becomes worth listening to, as one's intuition will guide thee. For love is so gentle, for love is so pure, how wonderful to meditate, for it can be the cure.

Positive Attitude vs. Non-positive Attitude:

With a non-positive attitude, you are mostly closed-minded to life experiences and opportunities. You may find fault, judge, or dismiss the situation because of the form looking differently then what you expect or out of some fear. Having a non-positive attitude leads to stress because your focus is on worrying about what you don't want or staying stuck in the past which leads to drama, where you create a life filled with one problem after another. The next thing you know, you have a chaotic life filled with frustrations and a victim mentality. When your focus is on non-positives, you get into a place of worrying about things that may not even happen. What happens when you're worrying is that you get stuck in the emotions and have difficulties getting out of it. Is your language filled with what is going wrong, problems, what you don't like, etc? That's the non-positive approach-one hardship after another.

With previous hardships, the challenge comes in accepting and letting go of the past and allowing the present and future to bring easier, more pleasurable times. Yesterday is gone, the wisdom is here today and you can choose a brand new life in the moment. What we perceive as hardships teach us lessons and by learning from these lessons, we can stop repeating the same hard lessons. You can come from a self-responsibility place rather than a victim mentality, where you choose to look at life as learning lessons rather than from a place of victimization where you have no choices. You can choose to let go of the drama going on in others' lives so you don't get stuck in the story around it. You have a choice on how to take responsibility.

When your focus is on positives, you console and nurture your feelings, and make choices to get out of the unfavorable situation. You then receive clarity within or solutions from an expert so you can take the necessary steps to get out of the situation in a more peaceful accepting manner. With a positive attitude you are open-minded to opportunities and to life experiences. You see the beauty in all situations and appreciate the lessons accordingly. Having a positive attitude is more relaxing since you are focused on the moment rather than worrying about the future or repeating past painful experiences. Some key things to remember with keeping a positive attitude, is to have faith, unquestioned trust in the universe, stay in the moment, breathe deeply, laugh to lighten up and see the beauty in all.

Acceptance & Discernment vs. Judging:

How many of you have felt no matter what you do, you feel you are being labeled as good, bad, right or wrong? How about when it comes to your actions? How many of you felt that your words, actions or feelings were not being accepted? That no matter how you approached certain people you constantly felt judged by them? Do you have a challenge with having another person appreciate what you have to offer or with appreciating you? How about how you feel about yourself and in what you do? When we are hard on our self, it ends up being reflected back at us through others. The harder we are on our self, the more challenges we face with others judging our actions, words and beliefs. Judging stems from our upbringing and our belief systems where we have an attachment to something we have learned and held on to it. Judgment says I have my opinion and you have yours and my beliefs are right and yours are wrong. When you judge you are saying, "believe my way, not your way." This creates a wall where you are communicating "at" each other rather than "with" each other.

Learning to let go of judgment is learning about accepting people for who they are. It doesn't mean you have to buy into their beliefs, change your beliefs or even agree. It is about you having your opinion and others having their opinion and knowing that is ok. As you become more accepting and kinder toward yourself, you attract nurturing people and situations into our life. You start to demonstrate in the same manner with others showing acceptance and nurturing behaviors. When you let go of judging others, there's a free style attitude with life. You choose to accept others, allow life to flow and appreciate the simple things in life. There is this amazing ability to not allow as many things to bother you. You feel an appreciation for life, you feel blessed, and realize how allowing minor things to bother you is a waste of energy. You choose to focus more on playing and enjoying the moment. You come to have a deeper appreciation for the beauty life has to offer, taking time out, playing freely like children do. You are reminded to enjoy each moment rather than focusing on the attachment of the outcome. Life is so much more fun when you choose to let go of fixing, judging and correcting others. It's also more peaceful when you're accepting of others, open to learning and enjoy each moment with full conscious awareness. As you stay fully conscious in the moment, you see things as they are rather than projecting bias thoughts and feeling from past experiences. Staying in the moment provides for new life experience, giving you more pleasure and aliveness.

If we get into judging, there's an emotional attachment. This is where you can learn a lot about yourself and where personal growth can take place. When you're judging something or someone else and become reactive, that is a clue that what you are judging is a direct or indirect reflection of something you are doing to others or is a dysfunctional belief you have. The reflection is a mirroring to help you become aware and learn from it. This direct or indirect reflection is something that you haven't made peace with. Judging is another way of saying we are self-absorbed in our belief system: *Where we believe our way is better, good right, etc. and those that don't agree are wrong, bad, etc.* Whatever you judge you create in your life until you learn and feel peace with the lesson you're learning.

When you use discernment, you are operating from a place of non-emotional attachment. You realize you have choices on how you choose to experience life and you respond accordingly. Through discernment, what you are doing is coming from acceptance which eventually leads to greater understanding. When you attempt to understand the other person, your beliefs kick in which is more self-focused. From acceptance, we honor other's perceptions whether or not we agree with the opinion of others is not important. What we are doing is opening up our minds and allowing rather than coming from a place of judging and labeling. The process of accepting is the first tool to building peace and learning teamwork. Eventually you will get to a point of just accepting the situation for what it is and what it's not.

Self-Belief vs. Self Doubts:

When you're insecure about certain areas in your life, you have the choice to move forward and get beyond your insecurities or stay stuck in them. Insecurities are one of the biggest reasons that people feel stuck in life, don't move forward or feel unworthy. Feeling stuck is from an outdated belief that keeps pushing to be transformed into a healthier belief. Your familiarity with it and your lack of commitment keeps you stuck. The desire is there yet the will is not strong enough to transform it. This insecurity creates a domino effect with the remaining of the 8 common distractions resulting in some form of struggle. The problems will continue until either you go through some major struggles emotionally, mentally or physically or you 'wake up to the realization of what you are doing' and commit to transformation. Commitment is the first step toward releasing old beliefs that hinder or hold you back in life.

Taking action to move through these areas of self-doubt is crucial. Do you sit and worry, feel sorry for yourself, play self-pity, stay stuck and focus on the areas you feel insecure with? Or alternatively, do you get insight through tuning in to see what you're insecure about? Sometimes our self-doubts come from forcing desired goals to come into fruition. The focus in more on getting the goal than it is on strengthening the inner being so we are ready for that goal. When the goal is not attained within a chosen time frame, we go through a phase of self-doubt. We doubt our ability and our self. Insecurities often make us doubt our abilities. The best thing is to get beyond the insecurity to a more secure place within. You can use insecurities as a reason to seek answers in the area of your job or life where you are experiencing self-doubts. Affirmations, discussed in Chapter one, are wonderful tools to shift beliefs and thereby release self-doubts. This can be an opportunity to realize you are worthy even with mistakes. Trust your self-worth more than your insecurities.

When attaining desired goals, there are two ways to go about getting them - working hard or playing smart.

Working hard comes from a control–forcing place. It's where you over-do or try to make things happen that are beyond your ability or timing. Trying to control or make things happen occurs sooner when impatience kicks in. Where you feel what you choose to have is taking longer to attain. There is a belief system here that says something like: "I will do something to make it happen sooner since it is taking way too long to materialize." Coming from a forcing or controlling place to make something materialize prior to the proper timing is only going to cause unpleasant emotions.

What is more important at this juncture is to breath, surrender to GOD, and choose acceptance to release the controlling hold you have on the outcome. When you released the controlling hold of the outcome, meditate to quiet the mind chatter and calm the emotions. As you focus on gratitude and open your heart your attention will shift from human control to inner spirit being. Connect your spirit being to GOD-The Universe, observe the situation and listen for clarity and greater understanding. You may get insights on blocks occurring from old paradigms- *belief systems no longer appropriate in your current life.* It is important sometimes to 'be' before you can 'do.' In other words, to come from a place of patience and listening for guidance before taking the necessary pro-active steps. Otherwise it's like having a road map and not knowing where you're going. Driving and hitting dead ends, going to places you didn't choose to go, or driving and getting lost.

There may be more lessons to learn before you can move on to the next phase in your life. The clarity and greater understanding may come in that moment or latter on. When you have completed the lessons and acquired enough wisdom to move on to the next phase, you will receive the clarity and greater understanding. The steps of how, where and when will be shown through GOD-The Universe. The messages come in a variety of ways, within, through people, in books, while watching a movie, and even a bill board. Receiving messages in this manner can seem so mystical.

EFFECTIVE STEPS TO ATTAINING *GOALS* WITH MORE ENJOYMENT:

1) Believe in yourself
2) Write what the desired goal would look like using positive wordings as if you already have it
3) Feel what it would feel like to have the desired goal
4) List the benefits to help you stay self motivated
5) Talk to educated people in the area of desire
6) Have faith and trust
7) Allow without forcing universal timing or trying to control the outcome
8) Enjoy, play and laugh to help let go of any stress
9) Stay alert and listen for guidance
10) Know you have receive the desired goal

I enjoy watching young children play because most have such an adventurous spirit. They have this amazing ability to use their imagination and create without limitations. They have the ability to think out-of-the-box when it comes to the unknown and enjoy new activities. If we as adults would choose to rediscover our own child-like creativity, we would be less intense with life, relax and play, and be free of judgments and limitations. As you move more into spiritual enlightenment goals start to shift into intentions. Goals come from human desire sometimes forgetting about the grand plan GOD has in store for you and setting intentions includes GOD's plan. As a spirit being when you set an intention or choice of what you would like to create in your life, you come from a place of self-confidence and inner strength. You have this inner knowing and belief that you can attain the outcome and move forward in life as if you already have it. This helps you stay in trust and faith as you listen for guidance.

Unlimited Potentials vs. Limitations:

A focus on limitations, is when you focus your thoughts on insufficiencies, narrow mindedness, and literally, lack. The human mind is more limited in perspective than the GOD-The Universe which is unlimited. The human mind bases things on the past failures and successes. It also includes self-esteem from those results, comprised of self-doubts and self-assurance. With the perceived failures, you focus is on what *won't* work, a limited focus, rather than on the unlimited possibilities that can work. Limited focus has bias thinking, preventing you from seeing unlimited potentials. Have you ever been in a brainstorming meeting where you are asked to come up with ideas or solutions? In the midst of voicing these solutions, have you experienced people saying that your ideas or solutions won't work? If so, what is going on is negating possibilities. If we are seeing from a tunnel vision, what is right in front of us based on our previous experiences or on what we currently choose to know, we are limiting our selves. Many non-effective approaches come out of non-positive thinking and a limited narrow view.

If we look at inventors, we will come to understand what unlimited potential is all about. Inventors look at a challenge and come up with a solution. They see beyond what is right in front of them, utilizing creativity to discover new ways to current paradigms. Inventors come from a 'what will' work mentality rather than from past experiences, judging, or limited human perspectives. In the process of discovery, they stay open to opportunities and innovative ways of creating things. They don't get caught up in failing, narrow-minded thinking and bias. In each moment in life if we initially use limited thoughts, we come from a limited perspective of what is currently known to us. The ability to shift our attention from the human limited perspective into unlimited potential, we start to open up to creative expression and expansiveness. If we were to transfer this process to our day-to-day life we would be able to take more risks in life with enjoyment. We would see the changes we are facing in our day-to-day life in a more positive manner and have an adventurous spirit. An effective approach is to go beyond the limitations by staying open minded and looking at broader, unknown possibilities: *To use your heart and imagination for creating and the mind for processing and planning the action steps.* One without the other is not as effective as both utilized together.

Obstacles perceived as Challenges vs. Problems:

Obstacles can be perceived as problems or as challenges. When we perceive obstacles as problems, we are carrying emotional baggage that can weigh us down. Can you imagine putting all your worries into a huge piece of luggage and carrying it around wherever you go? You'd get exhausted within a very short period of time. Well it's the same thing with storing it in your body through the thoughts and feelings, consistently thinking of the worst scenario or things that haven't occurred as yet and worrying as if it will. When we worry about something, we are focusing on failing or things not working out as we expected. When there is an *expectation* on receiving something, the majority of the time, disappointment follows. This is because the *expectation* has an attachment with it. The attachment has a hold on specifics of what you want and a control on the outcome. As a result, frustration arises when the *expectation* doesn't happen exactly as planned.

When we *anticipate* something happening, we don't have such a hold on the specifics or on the way we have to have it. There is more of a flow by allowing things to happen more naturally. You allow the outcome to transpire based on intention and desire. Since there is no hold on the specifics, you experience more acceptance and gratitude with what does arise in the outcome. Many times, I have heard and seen for myself, as well as for many people, how the outcomes are usually better. This is because by letting go of the hold on specifics, you are better prepared to experience beyond what you currently know. Specifics have a current focus on what is known based on what the mind knows in that moment. By letting go of the specifics, you are experiencing possibilities beyond current knowing.

When you perceive obstacles as problems, you are focusing more on the problem than you are on the solution. You are confronted with emotional attachment of *"what you don't want,"* thereby attracting more problems. With the continual focus on the problems, you get emotionally drained and feel exhausted. You waste so much time and energy on the *don't wants that you feel 'stuck'*. This results in procrastination and possibly quitting all together. When you perceive obstacles as challenges, you focus on solutions to help overcome the obstacle embracing any discomforting emotions. The focus is to comfort yourself and to find answers to resolve the obstacle. This process allows for resolution through pro-action, creating a more fulfilling means of attainment.

If you put your attention on worrying, you create greater feelings that things will not go as planned, and focusing on the 'don't wants' rather than the positive desires. As a result, you attract more problems and experience greater feelings of despair. Here is a fun exercise: write down one area that you are worried about and then hide the paper. Now let go of worrying about that area that you wrote down for 1 week. After the week was up, pull out the paper and read it. You may be quite surprise saying, "how silly wasting so much energy worrying about what I wrote." What you worry about will probably never even happen. Decide not to put so much energy on worrying, and more on faith and trust. Chose from that moment forward to believe in the best rather than the worst. This awareness will give you more enjoyment with life. I enjoyed hearing a student in class share, *"God grant me the courage to accept the things I cannot change, to change the things I can and the wisdom to know the difference."*

Having a commitment to stay positive, to have a positive focus, to believe in yourself and nurture yourself is the greatest gift you can give with regard to your well-being. This way you are bringing forth your greatest ability with every proactive step you take. With trust you know things happen for positive reasons and if it is meant for you to know why things happened the way they did, you eventually will become aware. You apply active listening, have patience and faith that the guidance of what to do next will come when necessary. Through experience of letting go of the hold on figuring things out, you become more relaxed.

In this relaxed state, you are more receptive to hearing

GOD's guidance than when you are stressed. When you are stressed your mind is over active, your emotions are chaotic and your body is unsettled. All that you will get from this stressed out place is fear based answers- what you *don't want*. From this stressed out place, it is necessary to breathe deeply, quiet the mind chatter, calm the emotions and relax the body. Then you can reconnect to GOD in a more relaxed state and be open for proper clear guidance.

TIME-WASTERS & LACK OF ORGANIZATION:

Time-wasters and lack of organization are common stress factors. It cause lots of stress when you let time control your life rather than respect it for what it is, a tool for honoring commitments. Effective time management is organizing your time so that you utilize it in the most productive way thus eliminating time wasters. Some of these time wasters are negative people, worrying about a particular area in your life, working harder versus working smarter; putting too much time into things you don't understand or have the answers to, ineffective organizational skills, fears, and destructive behaviors. Time wasters take valuable time out of your otherwise productive schedules. By learning your time wasters, you are able to eliminate them, be more efficient, and have more time on your hands to enjoy life by living a balanced life.

You may hear people allowing time to control them. Where they feel overwhelmed and rushed with getting somewhere or doing something that they don't take the time out to relax. The key word is CONTROL. When you let time control you rather than have freedom with it, you become more stressed, frustrated and impatient when things don't happen in the time frame you would like it to. Having freedom with time doesn't mean you are not responsible rather it is releasing the hold of time-the clock- and staying present in the moment relaxed as you enjoy each task at hand.

Examples of common time-wasters are:

Overly high standards

•

Assuming others' responsibilities

•

The desire to please others.

•

Lack of organization.

•

Constant interruptions.

•

Lots of trivial activities.

•

Procrastination.

•

Fears: failing, rejection, unknown

•

Negativity

•

Taking on other people's chores

•

'Living' in the past

•

Focusing too much on the future

Below are 15 suggestions to help you overcome your common time-wasters and become more organized.

- **Set personal focus outcomes and see benefits**

Be a co-creator in your life. Discover what makes you happy and be proactive in creating it. Some people flounder around not knowing their true heart desires in life. They just go with the flow, hoping fate or luck will bring them their success. As a result, they don't feel a sense of fulfillment. In order to achieve the results you desire it is imperative to know what your heart desires. The initial step in setting intentions is to listen to your heart and use imagination and discover what you are choosing to experience. Make sure it is in alignment with your purpose in life. When determining what you wish to experience in life, having clarity enhances attainment. This is where the heart and imagination come into play.

Many times the form will look different than it would if you started from a mental perspective. Setting goals from an emotional perspective is different than setting intentions from a inner spirit being perspective. When you view situations from an emotional perspective, it comes out of human ego desires which may not be part of your true purpose. When you set intentions you take the ego desire out, which is more 'me' focused, and shift the attention more inwardly to what is in alignment with your purpose, a 'universal' focused approach. If you think about buying a car, you may start out with mental ideas to assist in determining which car to buy. Things like, good gas mileage, low maintenance, safety, reliability and price. Then the emotions kick in as you drive the variety of cars and end up with added options like an expensive compact disc player, certain color, sun roof and so on. By following emotions, fears may come up with regard to the extra expense and other factors contributing to you adding new features to the car. Whereas, by connecting to GOD, the decision may be more from what is for the highest good for you, family if any, and the environment. Your focus becomes what is the highest and best in the car selection.

You may even end up buying an economy car rather than a racecar that feeds the ego's human desire to stay young.

When we create intentions in our life and choose to include the universe in the plan, then we are flowing as one with all. When we create goals in our life and we choose to include what is best only for one self, we are coming from a more selfish place. Some businesses incorporate the approach of including the well being of the universe in their goals. This is shown through giving back to the community in some manner, whether it is financially or through service.

- **When faced with overwhelming tasks, break them down into more easily managed tasks.**

Sometimes a cluttered desk is a sign of a cluttered mind. Feeling so overwhelmed with all there is to do and not knowing where to begin. Some people start a project and then put it down to start another. Before you know it, there are a bunch of half finished projects that have a great start. Others take the easy way out by doing the easy tasks first, thinking the difficult ones may WALK away or disappear, only to find their minds focusing on having to eventually do them. Yet others may feel so overwhelmed they tend to live in the future of what it would be like to have it all done, never starting. Sound familiar? There is a solution.

Breaking down large tasks to more doable steps gives you a feeling of accomplishment. Staying in the moment with the task at hand rather than focusing on the outcome, will help you stay present and focused. This will allow for more enjoyment, learning and fulfillment with the task at hand. Keeping a list of the tasks to complete will help you become more organized. Prioritize the tasks in the order of importance, easy to difficult and due dates to help you stay focused and complete them with more ease. By organizing the projects in order of importance and emergency, you are better prepared and can visually recognize the ones that have time restrictions. Organizing allows you to get those main projects completed and provides opportunity to enjoy the fun and easy projects when you get to those. Making check marks next to the completed ones, helps you feel inspired to complete the remainder.

- **Determine your most productive time of the day—morning or evening. Do the mind boggling, creative and most important tasks then.**

Determining the most productive time of the day can be a tool to helping you get more tasks done in a timelier manner and have more time for balanced living. The way you determine the most productive time of the day is to eliminate the alarm clock and allow your body to get up at a natural time. If you get up between 6-8 AM and go to sleep around 10 PM, you fall into the morning person category. If you get up between 8:30-10 and go to sleep after 10 PM, you are an evening person. As a morning person, you are more alert and energized in the morning and tend to get tired, less alert and active as the 10 PM approaches. As an evening person you are less alert and active first thing in the morning and tend to be more alert and active as the day unfolds. As morning people, do mind boggling, creative and most important tasks during your most productive time of the day, the morning. This will help you get the tasks done quicker and in a more effective manner.

Doing the easier tasks during the nonproductive times of the day will allow for more enjoyment during the times you are not as alert. The evening people, you would reverse what the morning people do. You would do the things that don't require as much attentiveness in the morning and do mind boggling, creative and most important task in the late morning, afternoon and evening when you are more alert. Morning people can extend their evening alertness by taking naps. Evening people who are forced to work early can resolve their lack of alertness prior to 8:30 AM by taking 5-minute refreshment breaks to assist them in waking up as the morning approaches 8:30.

- **Complete unpleasant tasks immediately.**

If possible, avoid tackling the difficult tasks during nonproductive times. You may spend extra time trying to figure things out if you attempt to complete difficult tasks that require concentration when you are not as alert. Do the unpleasant tasks first so that you're not thinking about them anymore. If you don't do them right away, thoughts may be on them while doing other things taking away the joy from the pleasant task and regretting doing the unpleasant one.

- **Arrange for some uninterrupted time each day.**

Arranging for uninterrupted time each day is a healthy way to take care of yourself. Taking time for yourself is a way to replenish the areas within that are feeling depleted. Doing things that bring joy and pleasure, such as exercise, nature walks, candles and music, walks by the ocean and dinner out helps to create a more balanced lifestyle. Sometimes the 'doing' entails just 'being' where there is no action except relaxing. Other times it may entail doing playful activities to create a joyful experience. When you take time to give to yourself, you are providing a very healthy way to love yourself. There is a saying: *work and no play makes one grumpy and sad each day.*

- **Don't get bogged down in menial tasks.**

If you notice you are trying to figure something out that is taking a large amount of time, a suggestion would be to stop. Getting bogged down in menial tasks is usually an unnecessary means of wasting time. Sometimes all it takes is sharing the challenge with someone with expertise in that area to discover the appropriate action or solution or even taking a break helps to provide clarity with a clearer mind and relaxed state. Taking the time to try and figure it out alone can be frustrating and the more challenging with receiving clarity. Letting go of trying to figure things out alone is a sign of letting go of control. When the mind chatters so much it's as if a fog comes and covers the answers. Surrendering the answer to GOD or taking a break is like lifting the fog. Sometimes the answers come right away and other times in a later time. In the midst of doing tasks getting answers to certain challenges can be like a puzzle. Some 'puzzles' are bigger than others and the answers in understanding the 'puzzle' may not be clear right away. This is where trust and faith come into play.

- **Avoid people who are time-wasters & non-positive.**

Time-wasters and non-positive people are energy drainers. Non-positive people who focus on obstacles as problems, usually procrastinate or don't take action to resolve them. They may dump their woes on others for self-pity and play the victim game. Being there for them to play this drama out, is not only a time consumer, it is also unhealthy for both of you. The appropriate thing to do is educate the person on how they're not getting anywhere through complaining and that they're responsible for their life and how he or she chooses to live it. Be clear that focusing on negativity only creates more problems, struggles, deeper pain and unhappiness. And by he or she taking appropriate positive action to resolve their challenge, will result in more joy, peace and fulfillment.

Choices play a big role here. Choices made to better one's life. You move on to the next phase in your life when you complete the learning lessons in the current phase of your life and peacefully move on to what follows. In Serendipity living, there is a recognized choice to move away from the victim mentality and take responsibility for your life; to improve it, acquire wisdom from the lessons life is teaching you, and live life with appreciation, joy and love. Your perception upon viewing each obstacle can change as you take responsibility for choices made in your life. There is a new awareness that the obstacles are present as learning lessons and opportunities. This can be major for some when you become a self-directed leader in your life. During the practicing transition phase, some can move through lessons more smoothly than others. This is dependent upon how committed and willing you are to breaking any destructive patterns and learning healthier behavior patterns. Remember mistakes help you learn and grow as you develop a new set of skills, making the transition smoother. During the practice phase, if you repeat a familiar pattern and if you look at it as failures, then there is more of a tendency to get caught up in the victim role.

Psychologists agree that it takes about three weeks to break a destructive pattern and approximately three weeks to learn a more constructive pattern. The length of time it takes to break a destructive pattern and learn a more constructive pattern is dependent on where the person is in relationship to the core belief and how committed one is in transforming those beliefs into healthier ones. Awareness of the destructive pattern is ninety-five percent of shifting to a more constructive belief. This is why some people go to experts in the field of endeavor to help them see the pattern and regain a new perspective. It takes choice, commitment, courage, persistence, strength and self-belief to become self-directed leaders. Commitment has to be stronger than the desire and the will has to be stronger than the commitment to develop new beliefs. Self-directed leaders live a more fulfilling life.

• **Mark appointments immediately on your calendar. Write reminders to yourself.**

Marking appointments immediately on your calendar and writing reminders are tools to help you become better organized. Marking appointments on the calendar, helps you to stay organized and remember the appointment as well as avoiding over booking. It is an effective tool to assist in organizing each day, prioritizing each task and motivating you to action toward success.

• **Write down your concerns to minimize the importance.**

If you focus thoughts and feeling on *the past or future with a failing mentality,* that's a warning signal saying you are on a destructive path that leads you into a fear-based worry syndrome. When you write down what you are worrying about and hide the paper, it helps you to release thinking about it. Seeing what you are worried about in writing is an effective way to help minimize the impact of worry. Many times the things that are in the unknown that you worry about don't even happen. The amount of energy put on worrying about it can be better used in more productive areas, than in worrying about things you have little or no control of.

Remember- *'yesterday is what made you today and tomorrow is not here; all you have is today.'* Yesterday and today's lessons have provided experiences to help you learn and develop wisdom to make you the person you are. What you do today is what will help you for tomorrow. Focusing on the now and taking the steps to make it the most fulfilling is a way to create happier, more fulfilling tomorrows.

- **Keep a time log to see how much time is spent on tasks. You'll start to see a pattern of time-wasters.**

Keeping a temporary time log is a tool to help you see where you are spending your time. Once you see a pattern of time-wasters, you can take the steps to improve on what you became aware of. This is a way to help you become better organized and give you more time to do the things that are most important or necessary for you.

- **Stop taking care of other peoples' challenges and tasks. Recognize and say no to what's not healthy.**

Taking care of other people's challenges and tasks creates a dependent relationship. When you try to fix other people's challenges or do the tasks for them, they will come to you to fix other challenges or do other tasks for them. When you try to fix the challenge by telling the person what to do, and the outcome is not favorable, you end up creating a situation where blame occurs. The person ends up blaming you and possibly himself or herself because it didn't turn out the way he or she expected it to. The two key destructive words in this pattern is 'fix' and 'expect.' You can't fix anyone because no one is broken and if you expect something or expect someone to behave a certain way, it only leads to disappointment because you're attempting to control a situation and/or person.

The healthier way is to recognize your limits and learn to say "no." You can be supportive with suggestions and asking questions, allowing them to take responsibility for their own choices. Some people may ask for advice and what they are really looking for is a soundboard, someone who listens attentively. Other times the communicator is desiring emotional support, someone who cares, shows compassion, gives and positive feedback in addition to listening attentively. When you offer advice, *telling people what to do*, you start to create dependency. If others ask for advice after feeling your support, a more effective approach in creating interdependency is in the following:

1) Relate the situation to experiences you've had, bringing it back to the person
2) Offer 'suggestions' only
3) Ask the person questions on how he or she can proceed forward

This process takes over the destructive way of advice giving, which is through telling someone what to do. Giving advice could result in blaming, dependency and followers rather than self-directed leaders. The healthier way is creating more interdependent relationship where everyone is self-directed.

- **Take time for personal recreation and family activities (balanced living).**

There used to be a time when workaholics were rewarded and people taking time out for personal recreation and family activities was frowned upon. It is refreshing to see that people are realizing the importance of living a balanced life. Living a balanced life is a way to reduce stress, live a healthy life and experience greater fulfillment. You can create your own wheel of life to see what parts are more balanced than others and where to put more attention. The most common categories include, family, work, friends, finances, exercise, nutrition, spirituality, education, and recreation. After you put your categories on the wheel, you then make a list of activities you currently do in each category. When completed, you'll see which areas require more balance.

Children are a wonderful example to learn about playing and being carefree, learning how to let go of attachments, sharing what feels appropriate and forgiving others when mistakes are made. As adults, we have a tendency to take life too serious and forget how to play. It is imperative to stop being so hard on ourselves and have an out-of-the-box mentality. Having an out-of-the-box mentality is a way to be creative, change outdated paradigms, and to be freer with our spirit. One of the steps to being an out-of-the-box thinker is to let go of the frigidness and perfectionism and to allow for newness and being different. Be spontaneous and carefree and still be responsible for your choices and actions in a mature manner.

- **Be flexible & open minded to others' suggestions.**

Being flexible and open minded to others' suggestions provides for new ideas and new perspectives. This allows you the ability to see things from a different view and possibly a more effective viewpoint. After getting information from others, you have the opportunity to go within to decide what part of the information given, if not all, can you apply in the area you are striving in. Being open-minded gives you the pieces of the puzzle you may require to move forward in your desired direction in life. As we move toward an open-minded approach, we let go of tunnel vision, stemming from a 'know it all' attitude. Usually the 'know it all' attitude stems from insecurity and self-doubt. Feelings of inadequacy arise, covering it up with superficial behaviors. Sometimes we have a belief that if we show we are knowledgeable, we prevent being labeled as not good enough. When we act as if we know it all, we close our self off to opportunities to acquire pertinent information. Choosing to stay open minded while gathering information from experts in areas we are not as educated, helps us to learn, grow and mature, and acquire wisdom more efficiently so we can move forward in a more fulfilling manner. With wisdom and age, comes the realization that the more you know the more you don't know. From this awareness, you choose freedom of letting go of perfectionism and being right. And through this freedom you begin to live life more carefree and playfully.

- **Be clear on desires.**

As you become more aware of what you are choosing to experience in life, you become clearer on how to start. Through clarity, you are better prepared on what steps to take and to allow rather than force or control the outcome. As you become clear, your communication and instructions to others becomes clear. If instructions are necessary, the clearer you are on what it is you are requesting, the easier it will be for the recipient to understand. If instructions are unclear, mistakes can occur and possible blaming can follow. This leads to frustrations and lack of trust. Being clear in your own mind helps you to make effective and appropriate decisions. Some steps will require individual action and other steps will require team effort. Sometimes during team effort, task assigning is appropriate. If you delegate to the people who are most qualified rather than merely available, your chances of efficiency increase.

Even though the fruition of a desired outcome may not look like what we initially desire, it's important to have clarity. Clarity is a self-motivating tool to start the process and lead you in the direction that is necessary. With clarity, you feel more confident with your decision-making, have a better understanding on what steps to take, and become more inclined to take action with a clear vision. Even though a future desired image may give you the big picture, it all starts in the moment, not from the past which is gone. Today created the tomorrows, the more you believe and stay positive the greater the tomorrows become. At times, the action required may entail being patient and allowing for situations, circumstances and people, to come together. This is where faith and trust comes in and listening for guidance. Meditation, as discussed in earlier chapters, is an effective tool to teach you to go within for guidance when necessary. In addition, meditation is a tool used to help you remove any belief systems that are holding you back from desired experiences.

- **Power words vs. Powerless words:**

In communication, it is not always what we say rather how we say it. Shifting your language is like a form of visualization, where *what you believe, you perceive and eventually you receive.* Your behavior and how you communicate that is based on what you are currently experiencing in your belief system. How you process the information is also funneled through your belief system. In looking at how we process information, body language is 55% of communicating, 38% is tone and words expressed and 7% is content. Our body language is shown through parts of our body, including our eyes, arms, and posture. Your eye contact can show the communicator you are present and attentively listening or in the future thinking of other things to do, showing a glazy glare in your eyes. How we stand, whether our arms are folded or at our side and hand gestures, can be used to gain or lose others' attention. Our tone is expressed based on how we are feeling. The content is the actual words being verbalized.

Using *powerless words* in your vocabulary give others the impression that you lack credibility and confidence, leading others to have a lack of trust in you. What you *believe* within yourself and your abilities eventually with enough focus you start to *behave* within these frames of beliefs. Your level of expression demonstrates these belief systems. Observing your vocabulary will help you recognize the insecure areas and any lack of confidence. Using *power words* helps you believe more positively in the areas within that contribute to insecurities or self-doubt. Power words build credibility, confidence and trust. Your body language, your positive words and your tone all will give others their impressions that you are confident and have credibility in what you are sharing. First impression takes about 10 seconds. Your body language, tone of voice and what you say all combined will either portray a favorable or unfavorable impression. Some people even base first impression by one's appearances. By using power words, you hold others' attention and create favorable impressions.

Below is a list of power and powerless words.

POWERLESS	POWER
• Should	Could
• Must/Need	Decide to
• Have to	Choose to
• Ought to	Prefer to
• Try to	Will do
• I Think I can do this	I'm Sure, I know
• Problem	Challenge
• But	And
• I Can't do this	I believe I can do this
• Worry	Embrace
• Doubt	Faith in the Unknown
• Expectation	Anticipation

When you opt to include power words in your vocabulary and in your belief system, you behave in the manner the power words define. If you portray confidence in an area you are feeling insecure about and use power words with, eventually you will convince yourself and others that you are confident. The more you practice power words, the more your thoughts hear them, more you feel them, more you portray them and eventually receive feedback from others that demonstrates the new reality. Power words can be used like affirmations, where we examine the area we are feeling insecure about. Upon examining our insecurities within a belief system, we discover certain words that when put together, provide the opposite to what we feel insecure about. These power words can be used both personally in our relationships and in the business world including, presentations, meetings, promotions, interviews or interactions with peers.

Distractions are created from a place of insecurities. How do you handle your insecurities? From a place of responding with love by going within or reacting from fear as you look outside? It is important to take responsibility in acknowledging what is for you to learn and what is others' lessons to learn. In order to discern, what are your lessons and what is being projected on to you, it is important to stay present and listen to *what* is actually being told rather than *how* it is being told. If you choose to take the necessary steps to remove your distracters, the rewards will be plenty, including professional prosperity, personal satisfaction, and an abundance of love.

This planet is like an earth school to expand in greater levels of wisdom and develop greater levels of love. Participating in the drama, controlling or forcing the outcome, judging the situation, other or self, and resisting only creates more distractions such as fears, limitation, insecurities, problems, etc. Observing the situation with acceptance for what it is and what it is not rather than participating it, will help you experience peace. Then you can choose to improve on what it offers. Allowing experiences to unfold naturally and embracing all provides for greater joy, peace, unlimited potential, self belief, and wisdom. With observation comes self-awareness. Looking at all situation from a WE mentality, which includes you, all people, nature, animals and the planet, rather than just a ME mentality, is one step toward living on purpose for the highest good.

KEYS

GOD gave us `Keys` to use to achieve our dreams.
These keys are talents, abilities, and a heart to love.
It would be wise to use them instead of abusing or losing them. - Angelica Rose

ACCEPTING THE HERE AND NOW

Accepting the here and now without questioning the why
and how; Believing in one's dreams to come true, without
becoming blue. Enjoying life, becomes one's focus; staying
fully in the moment and present in consciousness. For our
dreams to materialize, it is important to take it one step at a
time. Believe in one-self, for if not, it would be a crime.
-Angelica Rose

SELF-DIRECTED LEADERSHIP PLAN

The self-leadership plan is a tool to help you use your
intuition and if you choose connect to GOD to get a higher
perspective and to live on purpose. The self-directed
leadership plan is a creative way to help you make smarter
choices in life and expand your inner awareness. Smarter
choices consists of everyone benefitting that is involved, the
universe gains and it is part of your grand plan of why you
are here. For example, if you wish to be an opera singer and
you sing like a frog, realize singing is not in your grand plan.
Using creativity, I draw a special tree—the trunk, branches,
flowers vs. leaves, honey and bees as a process for allowing
what I call the intuitive-feeling side to open up in addition to
your logical-thinking side. The trunk represents the desire,
branches are the action steps, the flowers represent the
benefits to each action step, honey is the main reward(s)
from attaining the desire and bees are the obstacles to
overcome. Sit down preferably in meditation with the desire
in your heart and in your mind, asking yourself first if all
involved will benefit including the universe. Meditate on
this desire for a few days, listening for insights confirming it
is in alignment with your purpose. As you open up to your
intuitive-feeling side, you will start to create fun steps that
will help you enjoy the process toward achieving the desire.

Writing down the rewards to this desire will help you stay committed toward attainment of it. These rewards can be: *feelings of fulfillment, physical achievement, material rewards, spiritual attainment, etc.* As you complete the self-directed leadership plan please remember to have fun without allowing your logical side to take control and force you to be too specific, rigid, etc. On a sheet of paper, please take a few minutes to draw a picture of a tree. Next to the trunk write down a desire that you meditated on and received confirmation on it being in alignment with your purpose. Then use the branches, flowers, honey and bees to help you get in touch with the creative side.

- **Desire:** (List the desire and the action steps)
- **Benefits:** (List the benefits to each action step. Use as many of the senses, such as feel, taste, touch, see, smell, and intuition, for motivation purposes.)
- **Obstacles:** (List any foreseeable obstacles & distractions (chapter 5) and their impact.)
- **Description of the Reward(s):** (List the reward(s) you would like to experience from attaining this desire and the benefits to all involved including the universe.)

Listing the rewards is both a self-motivating tool and a process to help you get support from the community. The self-directed leadership exercise will help you get clarity on what you truly desire from the heart. Once you have clarity of what it is you would like to experience, then the pro-action steps comes into play. You use the mental side of your brain upon writing your action steps down to determine the necessary steps to take. Many times when we are striving for goals in life, we will face certain obstacles. Remembering the benefits helps you avoid procrastination and possibly even quitting. Writing a plan down is a form of commitment to taking the necessary steps to help you get there. It also helps you to be better prepared. It provides you with clarity of what it is you truly choose to experience and supports you with the direction to help you get there. A positive focus provides greater chances to attract what you DO choose to experience rather than what you DON'T want. As you follow the self-leadership plan, you put yourself in a better position to get your desired goal. I believe in writing in present tense as if you already have the desired goal and using as many senses in your words to describe in detail to help you to *feel* the experience.

Using senses is a form of visualization where you experience seeing, feeling and believing prior to experiencing. The more senses you use, the greater the experience will be. Senses like sight, feel, smell, touch, hearing and intuition. You can then become proactive with the action steps you wrote next to each branch.

- Take a sheet of paper and list the steps and their benefit to attaining that step. For example, Step One: what is the first step you will take and the benefits for taking it?
- Step Two: what is the second step you will take and the benefits for taking it?
- Step Three: what is the third step you will take and the benefits for taking it?

Continue this process allowing both the creative side to flow and then the mental side to provide the specifics. With the creative side, you are free flowing, avoiding bias thoughts and limitations. With the mental side, you are listing the proactive steps to take to attain the goal- *whom to talk with, what action is necessary, where to look, when do you choose to start and a target date for attaining the goal and how to get started. With regard to your grand plan of why you are here, remember the universal timing of When it will materialize and the Who and Where is part of the divine plan-who is going to going to come into your life to help you, When will this happen and Where? That is nothing for you to be concerned about. All will come into play as you take steps forward based on what you currently know. No steps are set in stone and can be changed based on what you discovered. Taking no action gets you nowhere. Taking some action gets you somewhere. It may not be where you ultimately would like to be, although it is a start to getting there.*

Below are some steps to ask oneself so as to assist in achieving the Desire.

STEPS TO ACHIEVE TANGIBLE DESIRES

- **CLEAR** – *Are you clear on what you want?*
- **ON PURPOSE**- *Is it in alignment with your purpose in life?*
- **LEARNING** – *What areas of improvement are necessary and how will you improve on them?*
- **TIMELY** – *Do you have clarification on the target dates?*

As you list the target dates, you may want to organize action steps based on importance. For instance, some steps may be labeled emergencies based on the urgency of completion. Other steps may be considered personally important and have priority over certain business or minor personal deadlines. After the personally important steps, come deadlines that are important to get done. Finally, which action steps can you take that require a short period of time and which action steps are more challenging tasks that require more length of time. Please continue your process of listing the tasks in order of importance necessary in accomplishing the desire.

TASKS TO DO TO ACCOMPLISH MAIN AREA
Start Date   **Complete** *Date*

Order of prioritizing
1) Emergencies
2) Personal importance
3) Deadlines (urgencies/time)
4) Short term or easy
5) Long term or difficult

By writing the tasks in order of importance, you get to see what is really necessary to do first. This releases some time pressures you may have put on yourself to getting all thing done. As you start to move through the list and complete the tasks, you feel a sense of accomplishment. Some people realize that they don't have to force to get everything done in one day. There is tomorrow.

- **CHALLENGING** – *Are they within your ability to achieve? Do they push you out of your comfort zone to help you grow and further develop?*
- **ATTAINABLE** – *Are they challenging enough to motivate you to achieve them? Are they easy enough to avoid overwhelming frustrations, procrastination or quitting?*
- **WRITTEN** – *Did you remember to write them down with their benefits? Writing it down provides focus and clarity. Adding benefits is a motivating tool to keep you committed to achieve them. Write your aspiration using the following.*

Be Clear
Use I or Me
Focus on Positive Results
Keep Your Words Positive
Be honest
Use as many senses feeling enthusiastic
Write in the present as if you already have it
List the benefits – what you will gain by having them

STEPS LEADING TO PROCRASTINATION OR QUITTING:

At times, we want something so badly we tend to push ourselves too much. If you find yourself trying to control the outcome, you'll become too limited in your focus, impatient, live in the future, and act impulsively. Below are reminders of the domino affect with controlling the outcome:

GOALS: *Forcing outcome*
ACTION: *Too focused, impatient, future tripping, impulsive*
YOU BECOME: *Confused, fearful, and non-positive*
RESULTS: *Sit on obstacles and become stressed out*

If you push yourself too hard to attain the goals, you will have a tendency to procrastinate out of fear, worry, self doubt or perceiving mistakes as failing. If the steps are too limited, you will not allow yourself to see possibilities that are more fulfilling along the path toward attainment. If in the process of taking action, you become too impatient, focus too much in the future or act impulsively, try to force the outcome, you could delay the manifestation process. If you continue this pattern you will become confused, fearful and non-positive. As a result, you will procrastinate or quit when facing obstacles and become stressed out.

Below are steps to assist in accomplishing intentions:

STEPS TO ACCOMPLISH MAIN AREA:

INTENTION IS: *believe in the intention of what you set*
ACTION: *Open minded, appropriately focused, patient, staying present and fully conscious in the moment*
YOU BECOME: *Clear, trusting, and positive*
RESULTS: *Persistent and have fun*

As you work toward achieving each action step that leads you toward your desired intention, you may come across obstacles and fears. They could delay your fruition if you procrastinate on taking action to resolve the fears and learning the lessons from the obstacles. Learning to solve your challenges and releasing your fears is difficult if you are unaware of them and blame others for them. Usually, when you are unaware and blame others for your challenges and hang-ups, you become angry and anxious, frantically trying to figure out what all this confusion and overwhelming feelings are. This only adds to more confusion, more frustrations and a feeling of "stuckness." Learning to recognize these angry and anxious feelings and thoughts is the first step in calming them. By calming the thoughts and feelings, you become more relaxed and get a clearer perspective. By staying focused and in the present, acknowledging your fears by feeling them, accepting them, surrendering and releasing them to GOD, you acquire a deeper sense of peace, trust and faith. As you stay present and listen insights will occur and those insights will support you in acquiring more wisdom.

The most common fears are *fear of the unknown, fear of rejection, fear of success and fear of failing.*

Listed below is a formula to help solve your challenges

EFFECTIVE DECISION MAKING

- **CHALLENGE**_____
- **GET ALL THE FACTS ABOUT THE CHALLENGE** *(detail, elaborate)*
- **GET ALL THE SOLUTIONS** *(people experienced in this area, brainstorm)*
- **LIST DISTRACTIONS** *(fears, limitations, insecurities, etc.)*
- **PICK THE MOST APPROPRIATE SOLUTION** *(with the benefits to that solution)*
- **DO IT!**

As you take responsibility for your life through strengthening your inner being, being proactive, and working through your challenges, in the proper universal time frame you will create the fruition's you deserve. Use strategy to resolve the obstacles by taking responsibility for your actions and results of them. The way to take responsibility for your actions is to collect all the facts on the challenge you are presently facing. You may not presently have all the facts, which I call *pieces of the puzzle*, to help you solve the challenge. In time it will get clearer as you acquire more *pieces to the puzzle*. Patience, persistence, time, and faith will bring you the missing pieces so you have clarity and understanding. When you get all the necessary facts, you will be able to come up with a number of alternative solutions. From that list you can select the best appropriate solution with justified reasons for acting on it.

Finally, have the confidence and courage and take the proper action on that selected solution allowing yourself to make mistakes as you learn and grow from them. You may start with smaller action steps initially, until you see positive results. As you take steps your comfort zone starts to get bigger allowing you to take bigger risks in life and enjoy greater returns.

HELPFUL HINTS ON ACHIEVING RESULTS

1) Visualize the desire and the feelings associated with it. See and feel its details and specifics as if you already have it. Don't become too focused or too picky on the details
2) Be committed to what you want by listing the benefits you will gain. This helps avoid procrastination and/or quitting when obstacles occur.
3) Stay in the present moment enjoying the process rather than future tripping, which could cause worry and stress.
4) Keep a 'Serendipity Focus' when challenges arise looking at them as growth opportunities. *Alternative is 'Murphy's Law Syndrome' blaming others and yourself.*
5) Focus on Positive Results:
   a) Emphasis is on what you choose to experience
   b) Gravitate toward the most helpful process
   c) Attract those that will be able to help
6) Choose not to focus on Non-positive Results:
   a) Emphasis is on what you don't want
   b) Get more problems
   c) Results are: Conflict, frustrations, fears, etc.
   d) Leads to procrastination, avoidance, and/or quitting
   e) Feel out of control and powerless
7) Believe in yourself and what you want without letting others' fears and non-positive attitude hold you back from attaining your desired intentions.
8) Surround yourself with supportive and empowering people rather than non-positive people and energy suckers who will drain you.

Visualization or imagery is a tool to help you attain the intention in a more satisfactory manner. Visualization is where you see the outcome as a positive outcome in your mind without taking any action. Visualization is an effective way to discover any insecurities, fears, self-doubts, etc that you believe within that could be sabotaging your efforts to attaining them. Through visualization, you experience insights through self-talk on any unworthy, limiting and insecure beliefs you may have. Discovering these beliefs is 95% to overcoming them by choosing to move through them and create a healthier self-image. Then you are able to focus more on the outcome rather than on the distractions.

- Visualize and feel the aspiration with all its details and specifics as if you already have it.
- If any self-doubts or contradicting beliefs come up write them down.
- Replace the self-doubts and any contradicting beliefs with beliefs that affirm your aspiration. Be gentle and kind with yourself as you replace the belief systems you no longer choose to have in your life.
- Each day take time to visualize your aspiration and release any non-productive thought patterns.
- Do the visualization exercise when you first get up and, as you get ready to go to sleep.
- Remember it takes at least 3 weeks to transform a thought pattern that you programmed so be patient.
- Surround yourself with supportive, empowering, authentic people rather than non-positive people who could drain you and negative influences.
- Be and behave what you desire as if you already have it and wish the same for others.

As you visualize and experience the desired outcome, remember that the outcome is in the future. It is important to continuously bring yourself back to the present moment, allowing the process to unfold naturally. By focusing only on the outcome, you are preventing yourself from fully experiencing the moment and the lessons that are in front of you to learn. Although some of the lessons may not seem fun, focusing on the moment helps you to move through them more effectively. Having the mind projected in the future only creates missed opportunities in the moment. Surrender on those things you have no control of. Stay free of trying to force or control the outcome. Trust and have faith both in yourself and in the divine plan. Allow the universe to guide you accordingly as you tune in by quieting the mind chatter, opening the heart and relaxing the body.

Meditation is a great tool, to quiet the mind chatter open the heart, and relax the body as you go within for divine guidance. As you meditate and experience life, embrace and release any distractions that hinder you from moving forward in a loving manner, such as fears, doubts, limitations, judgments, time-wasters, negativity, problem focus and power-less words. In place of focusing on the distractions, focus on the 8 enhancers, choose to believe in the outcome, stay positive in both your attitudes and focus and behave as if you already have the desired outcome. Stay open to the opportunities that come your way, allowing for new directions while in the process, as well as lessons to be learned for wisdom. Use discernment with situations and people that are not supportive of you or your chosen desire. Bless those that follow a more destructive path as they focus more on distractions, and move on. This will assist in staying focused and motivated to acquire the necessary tools to attainment of the outcome.

Finally, pace yourself as you take action. Remember the challenges you face are there to teach you lessons and to help you grow. Universal timing is different than one's own time plane for the fruition to materialize. *Remember talk is cheap. Action speaks louder than words.* In other words, *walk your talk of integrity, be patient, believe and know you deserve the best!* In our process of refining and developing more effective, self-directed leadership skills, we come to understand the balancing effect-knowing when to be persistent, and when to relax. In addition, learning to surrender to that which is no longer appropriate in our life and how to let go of control and allow. Through our process of improving our self-directed leadership, we begin to improve the four components of leadership. The four components again are self-belief, positive focus, skill development and positive attitude. Through our own improvement of self-directed leadership, our means of expressing also improves. It is shown in our body posture, language and the tone in our voice.

CREATING MORE JOY IN YOUR LIFE

Keep your life simple
Do what makes you feel whole and brings joy
Use your talents and abilities to your fullest
Try new experiences to expand your horizons
Honor your feelings, values, and beliefs
Surround yourself with supportive, positive, and loving
people in your life
Surround yourself with mentors and role models
Create a loving relationship with yourself and with others
Reward yourself with gifts- both material and nonmaterial
Continually educate yourself
Do affirmations on beliefs that are destructive to recreate
constructive beliefs
Applaud your self-worth which comes through growth and
wisdom
The difference you make in the world are measured by what
you do to improve it not by how much money you make
- Angelica Rose

CREATIVITY

Creativity involves a new way of looking at life.
It is full of originality.
Artists and inventors use it.
It is full of joy and enhances one's life.
- Angelica Rose

FOCUS POSITIVE THINKING

Whatever you stay focused on long enough you create in your life through experiences. As you keep the mind focusing on positives, master gratitude and develop high self-belief, you create greater abundance in your life. By putting all your focus on your fears and allowing them to control your life, you create lack and non-positive experiences. This doesn't mean you ignore, resist or act as if the fears don't exist. Rather you don't allow them to control your life. You release your fears by processing them and transforming the beliefs to more positive loving ones. Instead of just living life you enjoy life. Instead of letting everything bother you, you approach life in a more carefree, playful manner. Rather than looking at the ½ empty glass or the ½ full glass, you look at life as the whole-full glass.

In chapter 6 we talked about visualization. Visualization is a tool you can use to help you release a non-positive pattern and replace it with a more positive approach. Visualization reprograms the mind to create positive thinking, thereby feeling self-motivated. What you are saying to the non-productive thought pattern you created is that you are no longer choosing to focus your thoughts there. You are pulling out the weeds that hinder you from getting what you want in life and replacing it with a 'garden' full of what you choose to experience. Again, *whatever you stay focused on long enough you create in your life through experiences.* Here is a fun exercise to experience the positive impact of visualization. Stand up and put you non-dominant hand on your waist and your dominant hand out in front of you. Point your index finger toward the front of the room, turn from your waist up as far as you can to the right, if you are a right-handed person and to the left if you are left handed person. Turn without turning anything below the hand that is resting on your waist. Memorize the spot you are pointing and then return to the front of the room. Now do the same thing with your eyes closed, seeing the spot in the mind and feeling it. Come back to the front of the room.

The second part of this exercise entails doing this through visualization. This is where you visualize doing the pointing without actually doing it. Close your eyes and see yourself pointing in the front of the room and turning to the right or left, whichever is your dominant hand. See the spot in your mind and feel it as you memorize the spot. Now, go further to a brand new spot and memorize it and feel it. If any distractions, such as self-doubt come up, acknowledge them and continue. Still visualizing, come back to the front of the room, with the finger pointing and dropping the hand to the side. Now open your eyes and point the finger to the front of the room. Go as far as you can to the right or left, again based on which is the dominant side, and see where you are pointing. Did you go further? Take a few minutes to write down why you went further.

Many people come to realize that they went further due to visualizing that they could. *Believing* they could and allowing this free of doubt, judging, limitations, fears, insecurities, and any other distractions. They came from high self-belief and positive focus and thinking. This took the place of self-doubt and non-positive thinking and focus. Results were a positive outcome and success. Apply this in real life with new situations and in other life experiences. Reviewing the previous chapters, you will discover there's quite a difference between concern and worry when it comes to the way one handles obstacles and fears. People who worry see obstacles and fears as problems. They continually focus on it by dwelling on their obstacles and fears and playing the self-pity game. They constantly complain, blame, moan and groan, forming a domino effect in all areas of their life. Their attitude is affected, becoming non-positive to the point where they are not willing to change the situation or take action to resolve it.

The worried person has a 'Murphy's Law Attitude' where they stay 'stuck' in their problems and play the 'victim' game. The more one worries, the more their attitude is negatively affected. It has been medically proven that a non-positive attitude affects your health. One can manifest depression, headaches, ulcers, colds, heart attacks, and even cancer by repressing their emotions and thoughts in a non-positive way. These repressed thoughts and emotions are in the form of non-positive energy and when they are stored in your body and are not released, the body reacts by getting ill. People, who perceive their obstacles and fears as challenges, observe without any attachments, surrender to GOD, embrace, allow things to unfold naturally staying in the moment in faith and trust. They focus on their obstacles and fears with a 'Serendipity Attitude.' They look at ways to take action and resolve them knowing the challenges and obstacles are not permanent and that there are lessons to learn. Their attitude is positive because they look at these obstacles as opportunities for growth as they strive to achieve their desired aspirations.

List of results that come from a non-positive attitude:

☹ You focus on what you do *not* want
☹ Your focus is on non-positive results
☹ Your emphasis is on what you do *not* want
☹ You end up attracting more problems
☹ You have conflicts, frustrations, fears, etc.
☹ The results are procrastination and/or quitting
☹ You feel out of control and powerless

List of results that come from a positive attitude:

☺ You focus on what you do choose to experience in life
☺ Your focus is on positive results
☺ Your emphasis is on what you do choose
☺ You gravitate toward the processes that'll get you there
☺ You attract people who are supportive and caring

Comparatively between the two lists, you can see it takes fewer steps and more joyful energy when you have a positive attitude. You're responsible for your happiness and well-being. By letting go of what other's tell you to do/be to be happy, you are able to make decisions that are more appropriate for your life. Yes, you will make mistakes along the way and understand them to be experiences to learn and grow from, not as failures to blame another or yourself. Following after your dream, responsibly, no matter what the outcome is a major accomplishment in itself. Sometime when you're learning lessons, you experience uncomfortable feelings, by releasing them and choosing compassion toward another, you experience peace. Using discernment, rather than judgment, you avoid personalizing others' behaviors, thereby you are not affected unfavorably by their behaviors. When you strive toward resolving your obstacles and fears, you end up taking better care of yourself and thereby enjoy life more. Your attitude says, *"life is precious and I would rather enjoy life than worry about it."* By taking responsibility for your life and the obstacles you face, the decisions you make are more productive. Your life is run by what brings you happiness and well being because you know you deserve it. You assert your feelings and thoughts with conviction and compassion on situations and people who attempt to affect your happiness and peace of mind. Your life focus is on balancing your life in all areas.

You are enhancing a positive attitude and a higher self-belief, by trusting GOD and your intuition and allow it to guide you rather than allowing outside influences to run your life or tell you what is best for you. You're able to stay focused and present in the moment aware of your surroundings, experiencing them to the fullest and having more fun in life, rather than future tripping, worrying and playing victim to your circumstances. You are gentle with yourself if you mistakenly react in unfavorable situations with others, rather than discounting and internalizing your feelings or yelling and blaming another. Throughout the remainder of this book, I will be examining the less matured parts of one's belief system, which I describe as dysfunctional programs run by the ego. Through personal observation, you'll be able to detect and transform the areas within that no longer serve you. Letting go of old ways of thinking and behaving that no longer benefit you and your well-being and shifting your thinking to more constructive belief-systems, Freeing you so you can live more in *'Divine*

Love- oneness with your authentic self.'

EMBRACING THE MOMENT

Play and allow things to unfold such as insights and enjoyment.

When you are living more from ego control, you are behaving in a controlling manner; you act by overdoing, forcing outcomes you desire, grabbing and at times can become dishonest with yourself and others. You waste so much energy trying to make things happen that you don't enjoy and appreciate the simple things, such as nature and the wonders of love. Your mind is constantly planning, thinking of what to do next and how to avoid repeating what didn't work; making lists of steps to take to achieve things, focused so much on time and not wanting to waste it. The more you focus on rushing, the more you feel overwhelmed with things to do, and feeling like there is no time to do everything. By the end of the day, you could feel so exhausted you may start to eliminate things that are important to your well-being and bring inner joy. For example, you could do any combination of the following: stop exercising, miss out on the proper nutrients given when you eat healthy, stop doing some fun events and/or treating yourself with kindness and honoring your values and beliefs.

When you embrace each experience in the moment, you are embracing life. The mind is conscious and clear of any yesterdays and tomorrows; whether they're from unhappy experiences leaving concerns and unhappy feelings or happy experiences leaving more pleasant feelings. The mind is free of any future plans, predictions or figuring out future outcomes. Being in the moment allows you to enjoy the people you are interacting with. You have more compassion and acceptance of people's flaws and insecurities without personalizing or judging. You are able to forgive them for their mistakes and incompetence's because you accept their behaviors. With acceptance comes greater understanding. There is an acceptance of reality for what is going on in your daily life. Things you are able to change, you do with motivation and desire. The things you are unable to change, you surrender free of any form of control or resistance and flow with the life experience. You choose to be happy and you surround yourself with others who also choose to be happy and live a peaceful life.

POSITIVE CONSCIOUSNESS

Release thoughts and feelings that stem from the 'distracters' such as fears, non-positives and insecurities.

Listen to the way you talk and how you feel; If you feel anxious, it could be 'old programming stuff' that is no longer suited in your life. Accept, surrender, release and forgive as you acquire more knowledge. Let go of any form of attachments to support the process of freeing the old outdated habits. If you feel fear, it could be a warning, listen and act accordingly rather than live in it or resist it. Listen and follow when your intuition shares information, such as insights or opportunities. You will normally know it is your intuition talking and not your fear, by a feeling of calmness.

Focus on abundant thoughts, so as to continue to attract more abundance and enjoyment.

Focus thoughts on gratitude and throughout the day monitor the thoughts to see where they are. Check in and see how you are feeling. The way you are feeling, in addition to how well you take care of the body, will add to the vitality of how your body is behaving. If you have positive feeling, you will feel more alive and alert and if you are experiencing more non-positive feeling, the body will be more sluggish. Embrace the emotions to transmute the non-positive feelings. You are not your thoughts, emotions or your body, you experience them. So you have full choice as to how you wish to live your life - with greater joy, peace of mind and vitality or with greater sorrow, chattered mind and sluggish body. Of course taking care of the body by eating healthy and exercise supports overall well-being. Verbally communicate the intentions you desire in positive wordings and then release the thought from your mind. Stay present allowing the fruition to occur. Use your talents to your fullest and with confidence, moving forward with patience, focus, dedication, and enjoyment.

With practice, it becomes easier to trust that inner voice and act accordingly without allowing the ego control to convince you otherwise. At times the ego may bring up doubts, insecurities, fears, and even logical reasons, which are limitations. Staying persistent with your practice to solidify the skills that are being developed, will give you more confidence with your decision-making. As you become more confident with listening to GOD first and going within and listening to your intuition, you experience an internal peace, knowing you are guided properly for more joy, wholeness and abundance. You are able to release the mind from thinking and the heart from feeling unpleasantness from the past and future. You avoid overanalyzing or trying to figure it all out and instead allow things to unfold and happen. You enjoy each moment mindlessly, as you are able to focus on the experience that is right in front of you and make a whole connection with the people in your life.

As you continue to strengthen your inner being, positive focus and gratitude mentality, the ego will become less controlling. Ideally the ego becomes aligned, emotionally, mentally and physically with the divine self and the divine self is connected to GOD rather than separate, allowing you to experience a deeper sense of love, peace, joy and fulfillment.

Healing the heart.

If you have so much love to share and have been painfully hurt, rejected, misguided, taken advantage of, etc., you probably will have a protective shield on your heart. Let's examine the life of a protected, angry heart. You behave self-absorbed, selfish, and angry hearted. You may say "Why should I share with anyone, they don't appreciate me or my talents? I'll show people I don't need anyone, I can take care of myself," is typically the common thoughts. You live life through the eyes of defense and mistrust, ready and willing to react with vengeance or pay back. There is a deep need for love, yet you have been hurt so many times and thereby don't trust. If the pain is real deep, you may be caught up in the materialistic world, selfishly looking out for your own needs, forgetting about the other person's needs.

You may fill your deep need for love with material things. You may actually convince yourself that you're happy and feel fulfilled. If you are courageous enough to look inside, you will notice how unhappy you really are. As you come to a realization that you want more, you're ready to make peace. Deep down you desire to love and be loved. You will come to realize that by closing off your heart and protecting it from pain, that you are also protecting it from receiving love from both yourself and others. At times, you will initiate love with zealousness out of a 'NEED' to have love returned. The results have been that you are attracting the very things you don't want or feared you would get. This can look like opportunists taking advantage, with various lures such as money, lies, and phony love and you responding with freebies, undervaluing your potential and worth, and over giving.

You may realize what has been going on and play the victim game, becoming angry and closing your heart. This prevents you from openly sharing and thereby missing out on receiving from others. You end up feeling more insecure about who you are due to not understanding why people would reject and take advantage of your kindness. Then you feel like a victim, helpless to changing the circumstances and unsure of what to do. A way to get out of this vicious cycle is to make peace and realize the dysfunctional programs are covering up the real loving you. You are not broken, nor do you require any fixing, correcting or changing. Rather a transformation by making peace with those areas you let run your life so you can finally move on and love from a deeper more peaceful place. The desire to heal, forgive and make peace with those you felt betrayed by, taken advantage of, or misled you will take place. As you choose forgiveness and face the fears and pain that led to the closed and protected heart, you will come to a deeper acceptance, understanding, and freedom. You will shift your perception from those hurting you, a victimization mentality, to that of compassion and wisdom, no longer having any anger affect on you.

You'll come from a place of understanding that you are responsible for your joy and happiness and will no longer take other's behaviors personally. Your choice of friends will be based on respect, appreciation, and love, knowing all deserve this and staying open to receiving this. Your decisions are now based on what you choose to have in your life, based on your values, beliefs and level of joy. As you continue to honor your boundaries and take responsibility for your life, you will notice how calm you are when you send out love. The 'Need' for love will no longer be there because you have learned to fulfill that need by going inside and connecting with your higher self. Although you stay open to receiving compliments, affection, nurturing and love you don't demand or expect it from others because you are capable of giving it to yourself internally rather than looking outside to get fulfilled.

You may notice how anxious you feel when you are around people who are expressing unloving behaviors. Rather than reacting with anger or trying to get them to love you, you will notice how you make choices of not being around them because it is unhealthy for you. You'll become aware of both angry and loving hearts. Your initiations of kindness and love will be given on different levels based on how people respond. For example, those who have angry hearts and are protecting their heart will not be able to receive the love you want to offer. Your response may be in the form of a smile or a compliment. You may decide it is simply to give them space and leave them alone. The greatest gift for you is that you are not personalizing their current behaviors, believing you've done something wrong and thereby they can't love you. Or trying to fix, change, correct, or make them love you. With people who are capable of loving, you will feel a space of calmness where you are able to give and receive love in an open and receptive way. The love you give will be unconditional.

THE ROSE

Attach to every Rose are the thorns. If we focus on the
thorns- we focus on the pain. If we focus on the rose- the
positive- we will be enjoying life more fully.
-Angelica Rose

A PEACEFUL PATH ON YOUR JOURNEY

We all want to find a peaceful journey on our path in
life. A peaceful journey includes an abundance of
unconditional love and joy. It is easy to practice peacefulness
when we are on vacation or in a nature environment. The
challenges occur when we are surrounded by outside
circumstances that seem chaotic, unjust, unloving and
unfair. This is the time our peaceful journey tends to be
shaken and you experience chaos both internally and
externally. In order to have a peaceful journey on your path
in life, it is important to embrace all, master acceptance,
surrender the attachment to any discomfort, appreciate
daily and in the moment, express compassion and choose
goodness for all living things especially during the chaos.
Let's examine the difference between a "Soap Opera"
lifestyle and a "Peaceful Path" on a journey in life. Knowing
the difference provides the opportunity to discover ways to
change it to a more "peaceful path." I define a Soap Opera
Lifestyle as an emotional and mental attachment to the
chaos, unjust, unfair, and unhappy situations creating
drama and judgment.

He or she experiences unpleasant feelings and
thoughts from an experience which have a number of
unfavorable stimuli or from a person's behavior. This causes
a reaction-judgment with the situation or people involved.
The person starts to focus on changing an external part of
their life. There's a tendency to want to fix, change and
correct the chaotic, unjust, unfair, unhappy part in others
self, and conditions. This external focus will lead to a
victimization and feeling of helplessness, confused, becoming

discouraged, frustrated, angry, mistrustful and jealous of others' success. There also may be passive and aggressive behaviors and feeling of having to protect and defend oneself and/or even others; playing victim, personalizing other's projected insecurities, blaming, controlling, pleasing or overdoing. This feeling of helplessness will push one into a deprivation focus where their attention is on what he or she doesn't have and want. Our mind is like a computer, what we focus on expands and creates that reality. We can summarize the soap opera behavior as expecting results, which leads to trying to control the outcome and over doing. Trying to control the outcome, over doing and expecting certain results leads to conditions of want with a time limit of when and how you want it. The results are victimization disappointments, and feeling stuck when the conditions are unmet. Many common reasons for the soap opera behavior stem from a 'need' for approval, acceptance or love or blaming the chaotic stimuli for affecting the internal peace.

A Peaceful Journey is internal serendipity with circumstances that seem chaotic, unloving, unjust, and unfair. You set boundaries and find peaceful solutions with the chaos to take better care of yourself. With the perceived unjust, unloving and unfair situation, you know there's a positive reason for these circumstances, which leads to growth, wisdom and opportunities so you let go of over analyzing. You choose acceptance, enjoyment, appreciation, value, trust and faith with the unknown. You understand that if it's important to know the reason, in time you will know. The peaceful journey begins by practicing spiritual hearing, where you have awareness of your inner truth as pure love. Whatever your belief is, whether it is GOD, a higher self, Jesus, or any other devotee, you connect from a place of oneness in love and gratitude. The more you come from oneness of pure love and gratitude, the more peace, joy and abundance you will experience. There's also acceptance and compassion for others, especially when there is chaos, unjust, unfair and unloving situations.

The steps for a peaceful journey is pretty simple, yet can be challenging when obstacles occur. A peaceful journey begins when you hold self-love and acceptance. A peaceful journey continues when you choose to focus your attention on peace rather than on the chaos. Sometime playing music helps to shut out the chaos. You value yourself so others will too and you do loving things for yourself to increase self-love. You focus on unconditional love of all living things and choose awareness, peace, joy and abundance.

HELPFUL HINTS ON A PEACEFUL JOURNEY

- Practice meditations to quiet the mind and open the heart on a deeper level
- Practice being at peace with the unknown
- Relax the fears and surrender to not having to know the answers now
- Come from compassion with others and acceptance of what is and what is not. Remain free of all attachments. Attachments occur when you personalize others' behaviors and over analyze.

Helpful steps to create a peaceful journey in your life:

- Master gratitude
- Visualize desire aspirations as if they already exist now
- Have faith and patience for the desire to manifest
- To change an external part of your life, transform the internal belief that holds those patterns in place.
- If you become discouraged, quiet the mind and connect with what brings you pleasure. Allow the heart to expand and feel energized
- Observe all that crosses your path and sense from the heart. Ask "Does it lead you toward love & compassion, or move you away from self-love and self worth?"
- Observe and listen to your inner vocabulary that you use on yourself and others. Observe thoughts and beliefs to see if they're centered on victimization, negativity or judgment

As you embrace unconditional love and focus on gratitude daily, you experience a greater sense of inner peace, joy, and unconditional love. Increasing your vibrations so that you're in a higher state of love and gratitude is accomplished by having a peaceful mind, free of any judgments and past pain. A peaceful path comes when you live the 8 enhancers-acceptance, unlimited potential, appreciation, self-belief, positive attitude, solution based focus, freedom with controlling time, and power words.

FOCUS PROSPERITY CONSCIOUSNESS

As you further develop self-confidence and self-belief you are one step closer to developing a higher level of acceptance toward abundant living. The higher the level of self-confidence and self-belief the more open you are to receiving higher levels of abundance, inner peace, joy and unconditional love. Understanding that GOD-however you define it- is your one and only source and any form of abundance, peace, love and joy will start to flow when you relinquish the desire to control, force, make things happen and over do. As you experience a healthier self-image, you develop healthier boundaries. You use compassion and discernment with those who are antagonists rather than personalizing their 'stuff' and feeling unworthy or judging. As discussed in previous chapters, judgments are merely non-positive emotions placed on another based on a belief system. Judgments label other's behaviors that you don't agree with as 'right,' 'wrong,' 'good,' 'bad' based on how you perceive their behaviors. Whatever you judge, you tend to create a similar experience to that of which you are judging. Similar experiences will repeat in a familiar pattern until there is a peaceful resolution and you have loving compassion.

You can make peace by learning to take responsibility for any indirect or direct reflection, a mirroring of behaviors or beliefs, and resolve them accordingly. I remember a story told to me of a lady on a bus. She saw a man yelling at his children as they were trying to get his attention. She remembered as a child being abused and immediately labeled him as being abusive. She went over and said something, accusing him of being too abrasive with the children. He shared that his wife had just died. How he was still in shock and so were the children. She realized how judgmental she was, and how she was reflecting her own experience as a child onto this experience, and apologized to the man. As a result, she was able to make peace with a past personal experience in her own life. Learning to come from a place of acceptance, discernment and love rather than judgment will help you to avoid having to do the forgiveness work in the first place. Discernment is awareness without any unfavorable opinions from your beliefs. This awareness comes from knowledge, self-awareness, compassion, and higher levels of self-worth. You are able to walk away from unhealthy situations or people with love and kindness.

It's important to honor your boundaries, values, and desires in your relationships especially when you are selecting new friends and/or lovers and deciding whether it is healthy to have close associations with your parents and siblings. The healthier your self-image, the healthier your choice of friends will be. Those relationships that are not coming from a healthy place will eventually dissolve through divorce or dissociation. If your decision comes to a place of separation, dissolution, or divorce, it is important to make peace and leave the relationship with no grudges or hard feelings. Otherwise you will take the fears, anger, and resentment into future relationships. We're in a new era, what astrologers call an Aquarian Era, where peace and love will dominate rather than hate and war. You'll notice your relationships with others changing for the better, as you take responsibility for improving the necessary areas within yourself. You will notice how you let go of care-taking or controlling others. You experience inner peace as you forgive those who have caused pain in your life. Wisdom you gained will help you to accept people. It is their choice not yours as to whether they want to transform their behaviors. As you continue take great self-care and honor your values, the relationships you are in will either follow or fall away.

To have a loving relationship, it is imperative to learn to love yourself, to be self-sufficient and have balance spiritually, emotionally, physically, and mentally. To create harmony in the mind, emotions and body. Living as a spirit being in human form has a healthy, loving, personal ethical belief system. There is a high regard for all living things including the environment and animals and takes responsibility to do his and her part to care for all. You can improve emotional well being, mental health and physical vitality to create harmony. The emotional part represents internal unconditional love, self-respect, and a feeling of worthiness. The physical part is taking care of oneself through regular exercise and choosing a healthy diet. The mental part is quieting the mind chatter, choosing positive focus and positive thinking and continued education for knowledge.

As you become healthy and whole, your relationships with others become healthier and whole. You respond to situations and experiences with a loving heart peaceful heart. You choose a Serendipitous life which includes, peace over being right, teamwork over self-absorbed focus, surrendering over controlling, allowing over forcing, freeing your hold on attachments over attaching, acceptance over judging, and joy over complaining. I feel the true meaning of unconditional loving relationships is the ability to come from an authentic genuine space of inner unconditional love and acceptance. An honest place where you walk your talk and share from your heart out of a desire to do so rather than a need for returned love. There's quite a difference between the 'need' for love and 'sharing' love. The 'need' for love comes from a lack of love where you feel unfulfilled within. 'Sharing' love comes from a feeling of abundance of love within and a choosing to share a loving relationship with another.

It is not selfish to love yourself and take care of yourself.

A FRIEND

One who knows you and still likes you.
One who respects and accepts you.
Is supportive and encourages you to grow.
You can trust and knows you deserve the best.
Lives and plays in the moment.
A friend is true and loves unconditionally
-Angelica Rose

RELATIONSHIP BUILDING

Relationships consist of both your beliefs and other beliefs. Beliefs stem from healthy beliefs that make you feel confident and possibly dysfunctional beliefs that can discount your self-worth. These beliefs have an internal web and at the core have a root core belief. Some beliefs you are aware of on a conscious level and others are unconscious. These beliefs came from your parents, school, peers, friends etc. that you chose to take on as truth and live by. So now when you combine your beliefs with another in a relationship, you create a complex dynamic set of beliefs. The beliefs that are the most dominant in your current life, the ones that serve your overall well-being and those that don't, will dictate how healthy your relationships will be. The more unhealthy beliefs you release, the healthier the relationships become. Beliefs chatter in our mind for attention. If we give power to the unhealthy beliefs, without transforming them to healthier beliefs, we create this 'illusion of this belief' and project it onto others. Our focus is more self-absorbed with these hindering and outdated beliefs because of the control we let them have on our life.

A self-absorbed belief likes to be right and focuses on self-importance. It likes to run the show and so it acts as if what it's showing is more truthful than divinity. Human control stems from a self-absorbed belief with feelings of *separation and self-doubt*. From this place you start to look outside for something to fulfill a void. Your interactions come from a belief of "what is in it for me"-a conditional form of giving with an expectation of return. And when you don't receive, there's a tendency to personalize it as a form of rejection, which leads to behaviors of mistrust, anger, hostility, reactions and defensiveness.

Dysfunctional beliefs are destructive and leads to much suffering between those involved. If an intimate relationship consists of many dysfunctional beliefs, you'll find extreme opposites of polarity. This polarity may look like one person controlling and manipulating the relationship and the other playing the victim role, allowing the destructive behavior; both people coming from a lack of self-esteem and respect for self and the other. This type of relationship will continue from an ego level, until either party decides to stop the pattern. At that point, the beginning stages of developing a higher level of self-esteem can occur. Resentment only builds as a result of this type of interaction, leading to reactive behaviors. The mistrust and controlling tendencies may continue until there is forgiveness and peace. With forgiveness comes deeper peace from going within and transforming those dysfunctional beliefs. Now you start to walk the path of unconditional love. Authentic unconditional love comes from a place of honoring, respecting, and accepting. As you strengthen your inner being, you develop healthier beliefs and a higher self-esteem and your 'need' for love outside yourself diminishes. The higher the level of self-esteem, the greater the love is for self and for others.

Ironically enough when you share unconditionally you end up receiving more than when you give with expectation. The reason is that expectations come from a place of demand, manipulation and control. This ends up causing much friction with the other person you are connecting with. When you share from a genuine place unconditionally, those that come from a similar place appreciate sending you a form of acceptance and admiration. Those that behave in a more self-absorbed manner won't have a negative impact on you since your choice of sharing is unconditional. Dysfunctional beliefs push the human ego to control. The human ego goes into a flight, flight and protect mode. It is very convincing and if you choose to follow it, you will feel more lonely and feel separated from your inner spirit and GOD. When you choose to follow divinity, you let go of the human control and the power of those dysfunctional beliefs. The transformation of these beliefs into healthier beliefs allows the human ego to subside it's fight, flight, protect mode-ego control. Your inner spirit becomes stronger. Looking within is literally looking with your eyes, soul and heart *within*. Upon discovery, it is the richest reward in this lifetime. You experience what it feels like to be at peace within: *To feel the inner joy and love.*

As you choose to walk in divine love you will notice the difference between genuine unconditional love and self-absorbed love with more compassion. You no longer personalize those who are not as aware and realize they are growing and learning. Reacting to them only contributes to their experience, thereby experiencing their beliefs with them until forgiveness and peace takes place. Responding more from unconditional love, awareness and blessing the people that are experiencing the 'illusions of dysfunctional beliefs through human control,' allows you to move away from that which is unhealthy in a more peaceful manner. During this transformation you're no longer allowing ego to control your life. You choose to let go of the 'distracters' that were impacting your life in a detrimental way. Feeling from a place of love rather than from a place of fear is so freeing. Remember, fear is your friend, and that when you bless fear and listen, you come to understand what is occurring in your present life situation. Through this understanding, you are better able to move beyond the 'chains' that have bound you and kept you feeling separate. By choosing to be genuinely unconditionally loving, positive and grateful in the moment more fully, it is easier to let go of unwanted attachments, agendas, or expectations.

When you are ready to have whole and healthy relationships, the dynamics change. You move away from a self-absorption focus- 'me focus,' to one that includes the other- 'we focus.' The relationship is more fulfilling, joyful and easeful. When you're around others that are coming from a genuine place and are comfortable expressing their feelings from a divine place, it is exhilarating. There is a sense of peace and joy with each other. The way in which each expresses comes from a true genuineness of caring, acceptance and greater understanding. There's a healthy form of compatibility that enhances the friendship and builds trust. When you choose peace and divinity, you look at each lesson from a serendipity focus. The lessons help you to learn and grow rather than from a Murphy's Law place of victimization. When you are facing challenges, you take appropriate action to solve them rather than focusing on blame. When you have unsettled feelings about a situation, you nurture yourself and embrace the unsettled feelings, instead of worrying and doing nothing to calm them. You choose to let go of the worry and a problem-blame focus.

Through a Serendipity focus your conversations, come from a place of talking 'with' each other rather than 'at' each other. Talking 'at' each other comes from fear driven place, where they are experiencing life from a place of fear and protection. The fear comes out in the form of attack and destruction. As a result those that are heavily in any of the '8 common distracters' live life with many struggles and stress rather than ease and relaxation. They communicate 'at' each other from a place of blame and self-righteousness. When we come from a genuine peaceful place blaming is not part of the conversation, since blaming focuses on attacking and peace focuses on solutions. There's quality time spent on hearing each other, mutual beneficial arrangements and solutions. If there's misunderstanding, the focus moves away from a 'ME' focus to a 'WE' focus. Thereby, there is minimal to no personalization going on, rather clarity and focus on what is actually being said. Because you are in the present moment, attentively listening with a choice of peace, there's acceptance of other's opinions.. And when you communicate you are better able to relate to what they said rather than what you wanted to hear. When we all get from sole self-focus to taking the time to fully accept the other person's point of view we will have a lot more peace in this world.

Through awareness you are better able to understand when ego tries to kick in and take over. You're more aware on how to let go of the ego control and surrender to a place of divine love. Once you have awareness that you are a spirit being living a human life of unconditional love, the great news is there is no turning back. Once you feel and experience this in depth, the desire is more to let go of ego control rather than to hold on. This is the most exciting and freeing feeling. There is so much life to live and the ability to experience this fully is exhilarating. What makes it even more enjoyable is finding others who are experiencing from this place as well. The impact of combining forces and experiencing from this place together is amazing.

HOUSE OF RELATIONSHIPS:

Relationships are somewhat like a house you would enjoy living in. There are many kinds of houses each representing the kind of relationship you have within and with others. If you're single, you are looking for the house to enhance your joy and to share love with. If you are ready for a companion, you're looking for the 'house' that's compatible to your lifestyle. With the desire to move in with another person as a lover then you are checking to see if this house is suitable for both of you. And Married people are enjoying the house and making minor adjustments. Healthy relationships will flourish as you develop a healthy relationship within.

You can look at the parts of the house as representing the various parts of you, how you care for yourself, and the way you view growth, self-awareness and evolvement. For example, the bedroom represents your intimate desires and emotions. The bathroom represents cleansing and releasing of the old warn out parts and paradigms. The living room represents the way you socialize with others. The playroom represents the playful child in you. The kitchen and exercise room represents how you care for your body. The meditation room is where you silence your thoughts. Some may have separate rooms for each part of the house and some may have combined them into the same room. The important facet of these rooms is how you decorate them. The house is best described by the relationship you have with your inner spirit being.

A house that is dark, depressing, dirty, broken down, full of fears, insecurities and haunting ghosts is an unhealthy relationship and requires major renovation. A house that is sunny, open, spacious, playful, feels warm and loving, and has some areas to clean and repair is the healthy relationship. Then there is the house that looks real inviting from the outside. When you go inside, you find plastic on the furniture, masks on the walls and skeletons hidden in the closets so you cannot find them. It is hard to feel comfortable in this house because it is uninviting and cold, and there is a feeling of superficiality. Which house do you live in?

The first and last house represents relationships where people look outside to others for the things they desire within, such as love, security, and joy. They may settle for unhealthy relationships due to low self worth or controlling relationships where they like to run the show through manipulation and/or lying. You may get involved in a caretaking relationship where one is the mediator of other's problems, feeling responsible for pleasing others, discounting and ignoring their well-being. These relationships come from low self-worth where they don't take care of themselves internally; there is a longing need for love, and a feeling of loneliness engulfs them. Rather than fulfill their own needs of emotional love, joy, and security, they will look outside to others to try to meet them. Relationship types will vary depending on the level of worth one feels toward oneself. As you start to develop a healthy relationship with yourself, you may feel guilty if you stand up for your beliefs, take care of your own needs and desires, and try to stop the pleasing and care- taking. If guilt occurs, in time it will subside as your belief in yourself increases.

The more authentic and genuine you are within, the more authentic and genuine your relationships will be. An honest place where you walk your talk and share from your heart out of a desire to do so rather than a need for returned love. Surrounding yourself with people who are supportive, positive, and nurturing, and including relaxing environments in your life, such as nature helps keep you positive and empowered. It is also fun to make a list of activities that make you feel nurtured inside and then make a commitment to doing a minimum of one of these nurturing activities a day. Feeling nurtured inside increases your self-worth and prevents you from looking outside for this nurturing. In addition, you will start to feel more empowered to take control of your life.

It is also important to honor your feelings and beliefs rather than discount and internalize them. When you have open communication in a peaceful and loving manner, you keep the relationships alive. There's more acceptance and respect when you take responsibility for your feelings rather than blaming. By taking responsibility for your feelings, while speaking 'With' each other, you both create a positive step forward toward solving any challenges and keeping the relationship flowing in a loving nurturing manner. In relationships if there is a difference of opinion, you work on compromise rather than righteousness or judgment. You come from a place of accepting each other's beliefs rather than fixing, correcting, changing them or unfavorable labeling. You come to a place of peace and through peace comes togetherness for making things work. Accepting other's opinions doesn't mean you have to agree with them or take them on as your belief system. You choose whether to be in a relationship with another based on compatibility of each other's value system.

Having a healthy loving relationship requires you to be patient and kind with others. When a relationship consists of both agreeing to come from a peaceful compassionate place, peaceful outcomes naturally occur as well as respect. You will start to communicate in a manner that responds from a place of unconditional love. By both agreeing to a peaceful relationship rather than one, it is natural for communication to flow and the relationship to be full of love and joy. When both contribute to the choice of having peace combined with a strengthened inner being the relationship continues to flourish.

In relationships when you are supportive and empathetic, you are relating to others' feelings without owning their belief systems or taking on their feelings. Being sympathetic in a relationship contributes to wanting to fix, correct or change something or someone which only creates dependent relationships. Staying in the moment, feeling the experience helps you to accept and enjoy in the moment from a new exciting place like a new relationship with no preconceived ideas. Even though you may be in a relationship for years, by looking at the relationship from today vs. the past, with an openness to exploring newness, you make the relationship exciting. This is what keeps the romance in intimate relationships alive and solidifies the respect and care for another in friendships and partnerships. Friendships flourish and bring out the best in each other when it is based on a solid foundation of unconditional love, a compatible focus having a choice of peace, inner joy and acceptance and respect.

LIVING AS A SPIRITUAL BEING IN HUMAN FORM

When you are living life from a conscious awareness of being a spirit being connected to GOD living a human life, you experience harmony emotionally, mentality and physically. There is this sense of excitement beyond imagination, trust and faith in the moment, and expansiveness of wisdom and depth of unconditional love that entices you to share with all. Your mind is positive and focused and clear. Your emotions are peaceful and joyful and you have this vitality and aliveness.

When you are living life operating from an awareness of human control striving to be spiritual, you sometimes experience a sense of disconnectedness. In other words, you let the ego programs run your life, which are limited in nature, experiencing struggle and difficulties in life. You experience duality living that is both positive and non positive, feeling happy and sad, being confused and having clarity, and exhaustion and vitality. You experience duality because both the human control and your spirit being are operating simultaneously. Duality starts to diminish when enough limiting beliefs are transformed; where there's an awakening to the realization of your spirit being, which is more unlimited in nature, connected to GOD running your life and human following. Developing authentic loving behaviors and gratitude is the first step toward transmuting human ego *control*.

The list below is some examples of authentic behaviors:

- Self-Confidence using your talents and abilities in the greatest manner
- Responding with compassion, love and discernment
- Staying focused and present in the moment
- Unconditionally loving
- Positive focus and thinking with a serendipity attitude
- Applying gratitude in all areas of your life
- Accepting others using discernment
- Abundant thinking and feeling in all areas of your life
- Appreciating everything rather than take life for granted
- Responding to insecurities with positive, complimentary, supportive words
- Using active listening with others
- We are ONE rather than separate

Each of us are developing and growing at different levels. Some are more aware than others. Greater peace materializes with acceptance of all beliefs and differences. It doesn't mean we choose to do as they do or believe as they. Rather we allow each other freedom grow and mature at their own pace. Letting go of the old ways that are no longer advantageous or serve your well-being allows for inborn talents to blossom and inner peace, love and joy to flourish. As those inborn talents start to blossom, you become more aware of your purpose of living on this planet. As you strengthen the inner being, the alignment between your spirit being and your human being becomes more solid, with the focus being more on spirit and less on human control. You naturally flow *with* rather than *against* life.

COMMUNICATING "WITH" RATHER THAN "AT" EACH OTHER

Please take a few minutes to make a list of some non-effective listening and communication skills. After you have done this come back and read some common examples.

Examples of non-effective listening skills:

Body language
Turning away when someone talks to you
No eye contact
8 Distractions discussed in chapter 4
Assuming
Future-tripping
Self-focus
Ignoring
Doing more than one thing at a time
Mind wandering
Semantics
Selective Listening

Seven percent of the way we process information is content, the words that are being spoken. Fifty-five percent is body language and thirty-eight percent is attributed to context. Context is the tone of the voice and the volume. Looking at communication as a whole, it is not always *what* we say instead *how* we say it. For example through observing and analyzing the body language, such as posture, we could come to understand a lot. How do you stand? Do you stand tall with confidence or slouch with self-doubt? Body language being fifty five percent of the way in which we process our style of language, is a huge part of the total hundred percent. And it is only fifty five percent of how we understand and process information. That alone would not give us a clear enough picture nor help us to fully understand each other. With awareness we can learn to stand more confidently in a way that shows we are feeling more self-assured.

PROCESSING ONE'S WORDS

- **Content 7%**
- **Voice, Body Language, Context 93%**
- **38% Tone & Words Expressed**
- **55% Body Language**

EFFECTIVE COMMUNICATION

Communication is the number one reason relationships fall apart. Non-effective communication results from one not learning how to effectively communicate 'with' each other therefore, one communicates 'at' each other. When we communicate 'at' each other, we are coming from personalization and past hurt experiences. One may start with a pure intention of listening attentively to what the person is saying. Then a number of situations can start to occur. The person listening may go into past memories and experiences and give advice based on their own perception and bias thoughts. The person may project their thoughts into the future with what they would like to say. The person may pretend they are listening because they are not interested in the topic. All these examples are more selective listening.

Talking with another person may start with pure intention of understanding until our 'button' gets pushed. When our 'button' gets pushed, we bring up past unpleasant experiences into the present moment. The 'button' that is being pushed is defined as areas in your life that have not been resolved peacefully. Those unresolved areas start to trigger unpleasant thoughts and feelings and move us away from caring and understanding to personalization and blaming. When someone touches on that area that is unresolved, unpleasant memories come up and feelings of discomfort arises. We are focusing more on fears of getting hurt. We experience feelings of mistrust based on previous painful experiences. When we come mistrust, we start communicating 'at' each other, finding fault and blaming. We react in anger, expressing unpleasant and unkind words.

A suggestion to help you move toward communicating 'with' each other is to choose to take the personalization out when listening to another person and to focus on *what* is being heard. When personalization is present, selective listening starts to happen, where bias thoughts based on our own experience come into play. When you are present without personalizing, attentive listening occurs and acceptance takes over the belief system because you are in the moment rather than the past and focusing on the person rather than on yourself. As you move into active listening, you actually hear what the person is saying from his or her standpoint. This helps to prevent you from getting into selective listening. During a conversation with another, a 'button' may get pushed. When a 'button' gets pushed, rather than moving right into personalization and blaming, stop and take a deep breath. You can, ask the person to further clarify so as to help you understand the area you are starting to feel reactive in. The reactive place stems from pain and hurt. A place you have not forgiven. In this place there are leftover resentments and anger with particular people and/or situations. Alternatively, if possible take a break from the person. Observe your thought pattern, rather than participate and attach to them, and see what belief is being shown to you. When you learn to listen to *what* the person is sharing rather than *how* they're saying it, you begin to get a bigger picture on the unresolved areas of your life. You are better able to avoid personal reflection of these unresolved areas of your life that results in blaming.

Staying present and listening to what the person is actually saying is the first step forward toward accepting and responding from a place of love. With acceptance comes greater understanding. From this place you feel a more peaceful flow with the person you are relating with. You take full responsibility for your own unresolved areas of your life, which will help bring you toward peaceful solutions. Your relationships become more enjoyable, playful and positive. I have designed the LOVE formula as an effective tool to help in learning how to communicate 'with' each other as well as build rapport in our relationships

LOVE FORMULA

'L' in the Love formula stands for *attentive* listening. In the 'L', listening area we are focusing on the present moment. We are using our ears and hearing what is actually being said rather than what we would *like* to hear. We are hearing the *content*, the actual words expressed. So we move away from self-absorption and bias thinking toward what is actually being heard. When we're consciously in the present moment, we hear the actual words being spoken. We come from a place of really hearing what the other person is saying from their position.

If you don't stay present in the moment and listen attentively, you could end up missing out on some important information. You could also move into the past with your beliefs and start giving advice based on your own perception and bias thoughts from past experiences. When you give advice from this place, two things can occur. One, you can create a dependant relationship by the other person constantly asking for advice and you helping him or her. Or, the person receiving the advice can create animosity with you giving advice if the desired outcome was not what he or she was expecting. Both situations ends up being a lose-lose situation. Sometimes when people ask for advice, what they are really asking for is for you to be a soundboard and provide compassion. Refraining from giving advice can be a very challenging thing at times to do. Remember the 'L" is only seven-percent content out of the one hundred percent in the way we process information. With only seven percent in the "L", that is not enough to experience effective communication. This is where the "O" comes in.

'O' in the Love formula stands for observing, where we are using our eyes. What we are observing is the body language, which is the fifty-five percent. In addition, we are also using the ears for hearing the tone and volume, which are thirty–eight percent and the content, which is the remaining seven percent. Now again, with all that information do you think you would be one hundred percent accurate in understanding what the other person is saying? No, because what is missing, which some people have a tendency to avoid doing, is *verifying*.

'V' in the Love formula stands for *verifying*. Here is where we are solidifying active listening. You are verifying what you heard and saw for clarity purposes. To make sure you understood what the person was saying rather than your own self-bias thoughts or on caretaking. When we are verifying, what we are doing is using our ears to hear the actual words, the content and listening to their tone and volume. In addition, we are using our eyes to see the body language. Have you ever been in a situation where the body shows you one thing and the words say something else? Do you interpret what a person is saying from what you *hear* or from what you *see*? If you are present in the moment focusing and verifying on what you *heard* and *saw*, you will have a greater chance of getting what the person is saying. Also by staying present with the person you are more equipped to respond in a loving manner than if you live in the past with your bias beliefs and selective hearing. Body language is only fifty-five percent. There is a great chance of misunderstanding the person you are listening to, if you only observe with the eyes and live in your "head" with your bias thoughts. Verifying helps you clarify what you heard and saw to become better informed and understand the true intention. It also reminds you to stay present and focused on the person speaking.

It is easy for many of us to go right into advice giving rather than verifying, based on our own experiences in relation to what the person is sharing. Starting to come out of our mouth, we may express our opinions with words like "I will tell you what you got to do." This happens from a sincere place of caring or thinking we know better based on our *own personal experien*ces. If you get into advice giving rather than verifying, you are focusing more on self than the other person and on fixing their situation. Body language, content and context put all together help us in better accept their current personal frame of mind and feelings. When you move away from self focus to being in the present moment and apply active listening, you are more effective with the next step.

'E' stands for empathy, where you are relating from a place of connecting 'with' the person with love and compassion. You move away from sympathy, which is where one's personal beliefs kick in resulting in wanting to fix and correct the other person's beliefs, frame of mind and emotions. If you start to sympathize, you become a therapist wanting to solve their problems or give advice on what they are sharing. When you take on someone else's problems, you start to feel miserable while the other person, after venting, is now feeling much better. This process is a lose-lose situation, because even though the other person feels better, you started to create is a co-dependent relationship on top of feeling miserable. From a co-dependent place, this person depends on you to solve their perceived problems for them and you feel and own their pain as if it is yours.

In empathy you come from a place of relating without owning. It is as if you are saying, "I accept what you are feeling. If I were you, I would feel the same way, although I *am not* you." From this place you are better able to be a soundboard and create an interdependent relationship. In an interdependent relationship you allow the other person to make his or her own decisions playing the role of supporter versus solver. As a supporter you offer suggestions, based on expertise and personal experiences. This creates self-directed leadership, moving toward resolution with regards to attaining effective outcomes. After playing the soundboard, if advice is asked, then you do a combination of three things. In advice giving from an interdependent position, you *first demonstrate empathy*, where you relate to their feelings and thoughts with love and compassion. *Second, you share a similar experience with a positive outcome mentioning their experience is coming from their belief system and experience will help them to grow and mature in wisdom. Third, you question and motivate him or her to act on their decisions.*

When you motivate others to act on their own decision, you move away from telling them what to do to offering suggestions and allowing them to make their own choices. What you are creating here is more self-directed leaders. This helps you in creating a more balanced lifestyle as well, since you're no longer taking on other's burdens.

LOVE FORMULA

LISTEN
* Attentive listening; Concentrate Avoiding Mind Wandering, Interrupting or Constant **"ah-hums"**

OBSERVE
* Observe Body Language/Tone Of Voice/Face Expression With Your Eyes/Ears-Without Personal Bias Thinking

VERIFY
* Repeat What You Heard Using Some Of Their Words (Avoid giving Advice)

EMPATHIZE
* Empathize is *Supportive*; Observe The Situation, Accepting it for what it is and is not. Relate To Their Feelings
* Sympathize is *Emotionally* Involved and Commiserating; Feeling Responsible For Their Problems. Attempting to fix, correct or change their belief*s*

With the LOVE formula applied in your day to day life, there's more responsive communication, present and attentive listening, acceptance of what is and what is not and connecting from a 'WE' mentality. With acceptance comes a greater understanding. If we attempt to understand first, our belief system(s) kick in. If the belief(s) resonate with what we hear, we then accept what the person is saying. If the belief doesn't resonate, there's a tendency to move away from LOVE and into judgment. With judgment, comes righteousness and with righteousness comes blame, leading to a talking 'at' each other. If you start to judge, you can own up to it and apologize to help clear the air and make peace with the other person. Making peace helps to move you into the 'WE' mentality and responsiveness with the person you are connecting with.

If advice is asked after applying the LOVE formula, you can apply the following steps to support them in making their own decision. First empathize, which creates a heart-felt connection. Secondly, you can either share your own their own decision or move into questioning and motivating.

ADVICE:

- Empathize, Sharing Own Experience
- Question and Motivate Them To Act On Their Own Decision (Used With Challenges)

LEVELS OF COMMUNCATION

There are various levels of communication you go through when you meet someone and build a relationship. When you first meet someone, you talk 'small talk' which is unspecific and brief. As you build a relationship with the person, you ask more questions, share opinions, and reveal more feelings. Listed next, are the levels of communication you go through as you get to know the other person:

Getting to know the other person:

- Small talk
- Open-ended questioning
- Questions with a yes/no answer
- Sharing an opinion
- Revealing feelings more

Relationship building:

- Sharing deeper inner feelings with each other
- Discussing differences
- Tuned in with the other person, accepting to bring a greater understanding

PACE OF SPEAKING:

Attitude is also important when communicating. Your tone of voice states your emotions and whether or not you have a positive or non-positive attitude. If you're in a bad mood, your tone of voice can show anger, frustration, etc. If you're in a happy mood, your pace of speaking, your tone of voice, pitch, and body language will show it. Your pitch and the pace in which you speak are also a tool used to express your attitude. How you're feeling, will be expressed in your tone of voice, pitch, pace of speaking and body language. Your pitch may show more enthusiasm, your pace of speaking possibly faster from excitement, and your body language more jovial. A variety is more interesting and will draw people toward you more than a monotone or a tone that demonstrates non-positive behaviors. If the pitch is too high or too low, it will sound strained, and irritate the listener. If your pace is too slow, you can bore the listener and lose their attention. If your pace is too fast, it may be difficult to understand, thereby losing the listener's confidence, attention and interest.

Pace of speaking:

Too slow: can lose other's attention

Too fast: difficult to understand; can create confusion

Non-words: demonstrates insecurity, where you could lose the confidence and trust of the listener. (Words such as "um," "uh-huh," lots of "and," etc.)

Tone:

What you say and how you say it. Tone states emotions and attitude

Pitch:

A variety is more interesting and will draw the listener toward you. If it is too low or high it could sound strained and irritate the listener. Observing the listener while communicating, and verifying to make sure he or she is still present will give you insights on your pitch, tone and pace. Based on their response, you will have a better idea on how to proceed with your pace, tone and pitch. Sometimes a topic that comes across as mundane can be shared more enthusiastically through your pace, tone and pitch. Becoming more aware of the individual's or audience's attentiveness and interest in your topic, is a great way to build rapport.

RAPPORT BUILDING

Communication styles are the way people process the information that they are hearing. They can process it in one of three ways: visual, auditory or kinesthetic. Visual is someone who processes by **seeing** the information. Auditory is someone who processes by **hearing** the information. And Kinesthetic is someone who processes by **analyzing, relying heavily on their emotions or intuition.** Depending on the situation, a person can use one or more of these styles in processing. Normally, an individual will dominate in one of these three styles in different environments based on their comfort level. When you initially start a conversation with someone new, he or she may use unspecific language or business like words and mannerisms. Once you start to earn their trust and build rapport in a positive manner, the person will show what type of communication style he or she is most comfortable with in the present situation. The communication styles are listed below to help you understand how people process information. Through understanding communication styles, you have another tool to assist in building healthier relationships and rapport.

Communication Styles:

Unspecific:

Unspecific is demonstrated with business like words and mannerisms. You first start off using "small talk" until some form of comfort or trust is built. Unspecific words are used such as, know, experience, understand, think, decide, perceive, process and change. You can use the phrase, 'how specifically,' to start to build the rapport and learn what communication style the person is most comfortable within the present situation. For example, when you observe someone in conversation with you and they say, "I experienced an interesting situation at work." You can say, "how specifically?" This will prompt him or her to start sharing more in-depth. As you communicate and listen to the other person, observe their body language, posture, the type of words used, and pace of speech. In this way you can identify whether he or she is auditory, kinesthetic or visual. Pay attention to the words being used. Are they visual, auditory, or kinesthetic?

People that process information **visually,** process information best using the written format. As they process information it is imperative for them to write and see what is written. They use words in their vocabulary that demonstrates visual, such as see, picture, reveal, appear, illuminate, view, sight, glimpse, witness and imagine. People that process information in an **auditory** manner, process information best from hearing the spoken words. They listen and understand more so from hearing what and how the words are spoken rather than from visually seeing. They use auditory words in their vocabulary, such as hear, sound, tune in, expression, say, discuss, attune listen, resonance, noise, speak and talk. People that process information **kinesthetically,** express and process information from a sensation place where they enjoy feeling and experiencing situations fully. They process information from a place of feeling while learning and use words that demonstrate sensation, such as feel, touch, sense, aware, ambiance, process and experience.

COMMUNICATING MORE EFFECTIVELY

In understanding and applying the different communication styles, we are better able to relate even more effectively with others. As a communicator, by speaking the communication style as the listener, the listener is better able to understand and that helps to enhance rapport. Once the connection is made you can combine both your communication style and their style for comfort. With the different cultures, the ways in which each of us processes information and the complexities of our lives, the key is to have effective tools to communication. This world would be a more peaceful world, if we took the time and really cared about what is being said. The first step in effective communication is to focus on being fully conscious in the moment applying attentive listening from their perspective with a 'We' mentality rather than your own bias belief system.

Below are 20 ways to communicate more effectively.

20 WAYS TO COMMUNCATE MORE EFFECTIVELY

- Make sure you're speaking the same language-semantics
- Repeat what you thought you heard to make sure you heard the person correctly
- Listen attentively-Don't let the mind wander or do other activities
- Wait till the person is finished speaking-instead of interrupting
- Question rather than assume you know what the person is saying
- Define what you want & be specific in the way you say it
- Accept and use discernment rather than criticize, judge or think bias
- Allow others to have their opinion rather than argue or become defensive with others' opinions
- Be complimentary
- Use empathy rather than sympathy
- Be open-minded and flexible
- On unclear comments, ask questions rather than guess what they are trying to say
- Ask questions or make suggestions instead of telling people what to do
- Share their enthusiasm by mirroring their behavior
- See through the speaker's eyes when they communicate
- Avoid listening with your own biases
- Focus on the 'we' vs. 'me' to create synergy
- Respond in love and compassion
- Observe first participate second when listening
- Connect from the heart rather than just the mind

I CHOOSE

I choose to live by choice not by chance.
To transform with commitment, not make excuses.
To be motivated instead of procrastinating.
To be useful not useless.
To excel not compete.
I choose self-esteem not self-pity.
I choose to listen to the inner voice not only the random
opinion of others.

One cannot collect all the beautiful shells on the beach
One can collect only a few, and the few are more beautiful.

Too much of any one thing negates whatever special
experience might have been realized. If we surround
ourselves with acquaintances, we never fully share in
knowing a few people well.

If we surround ourselves with toys, we never learn how we
really want to spend our time. When we take life slowly, one
shell at a time, in the present, we discover the greatest
discovery of all, the person within.

When our attention to persons, places and things is
deliberate and steady, beauty within the object of our focus
shines forth. And we too are made more beautiful in the
process. So take time to smell the flowers.
-Angelica Rose

LIVING ON PUROSE

When choose to live life with your inner spirit leading more than the Ego control, you experience more depth in all areas of your life. This awareness is a blessing and is unfamiliar to those who aren't experiencing it at the same depth you are. You standing in truth is like a light in a dark lit room. You 'awaken' those up who are ready to remember their truth. The more centered you are in unconditional love the less affected you become with those who project their insecurities or needy feelings You have an inner strength, becoming a role model to those who forgot and come more from a fear driven focus and insecurity. Their life is more duality living and you're experiencing more oneness. Oneness being a deeper connection to GOD-The Universe as a spirit being leading your life in a flowing manner. Those who live a duality type of life live more from a combination of Murphy Law Syndrome and Serendipity. They live a human life striving to grow and evolve, thereby experiencing more struggles. Struggles serve their purpose as well in that they provide for greater opportunities to learn, grow and acquire wisdom. It is more about the perception of the struggles, whether they are perceived from a Serendipity focus or a Murphy Law Syndrome focus. If the problems are perceived from a Murphy Law Syndrome focus-a problem oriented focus, then more problems start to occur as a domino effect in addition to attracting any of the 8 distractions discussed in Chapter 4. You become more attached to the mental chatter-the story of what is not working and emotional drama.

If the struggles are perceived from a Serendipity Focus, you look at struggles as an obstacle, knowing they are there to help you learn a lesson, grow and develop more wisdom. You choose to live life using the 8 enhancers and feel more relaxed with greater inner peace. You move through the lessons in a smoother manner than you would with Murphy Law Syndrome. Both make you wiser, Murphy

Law Syndrome does it in a more drama oriented manner than Serendipity. Serendipity focus gives you the tools to learn lessons and transform dysfunctional beliefs to healthier ones in a more peaceful, calmer manner. Murphy Law Syndrome, consists of human control. You are living a duality life, both drama and peace, as a human attempting to control life. The amount of time you spend in Murphy Law Syndrome is dependent upon the level of awareness with regard to the dysfunctional belief you are transforming, your commitment to transforming it and your strength of your inner being. The stronger the commitment and the greater the strength of the inner being, the less impact Murphy Law Syndrome will have on you because your actions will start to shift into Serendipity where you move through the lessons of transforming the dysfunctional belief to a healthy belief with greater ease.

Surrendering the human control is the first step toward transformation. Then you can observe the thoughts to see what they're saying without attaching to them. The human control may want to fix, change or correct the situation. If you move into acceptance and allowing, you are better able to let go of the human control. As you let go of human control, the next step is to quiet the mind chatter and shift it to a positive focus and calm the emotional drama and shift that to appreciation. Letting go of the human control helps you to remember you're a spirit being not a human control being. Finally connecting to GOD and listening for steps to take to transform the dysfunctional belief. With clarity it is easier to know how to transform the dysfunctional belief to a healthier belief. The greater the amount of healthier beliefs, the more heighten awareness you experience. The rest gets easier. Life becomes more joyful and peaceful. You start to have a greater expansiveness with unconditional love and share that with all. You have this greater capacity of love and acceptance for all living things on the planet and a desire to get involved with supporting the community to improve what you feel called to do. NOW you are living on purpose, where you understand the concept of sharing. You move more into oneness and come from pure love and higher intelligence.

As more people awaken to the awareness of oneness, we will experience greater peace.

Meditation helps you silence the mind chatter, calm the emotions and connect to GOD as a spirit being, creating oneness. When you look within and fill yourself with what you normally would search outside for, then you move into a place of completeness. With completeness you experience wholeness, sending out love from a prosperity conscious place. You live life from a pure place of love and a higher intelligence as you strengthen your connection as a spirit being having a human experience and connecting to GOD. Alternatively, living from human control you experience a feeling of separateness. The human ego control begins to look outside to replace this sense of separation-void. This leaves you feeling empty and incomplete. This pattern will continue until you become aware that all needs are filled from within rather than from outside. Once you break this pattern of looking outside, the rest gets easier. You start to feel more empowered, alive, and a sense of oneness with all and you feel this at a higher level of awareness. From this new level of awareness you will attract others who also come from a similar focus.

The more connected you are to your divine loving self the easier it is to discern between human-based fear and divine-love guidance. One of the key tools is how your body responds. If the body reacts with anxiousness, you are being shown that you are following human-based fear. If the body responds with peace, this is a signal that you are connected as a spirit being to GOD open to divine guidance. Divine guidance has a natural flow with life, experiencing unconditional love, joy, inner peace, vitality, and prosperity. Human control disconnects from GOD, experiencing more struggles. When you let go of human-control and allow, you flow with divine guidance. You let go of human control when you stop trying to figure things out, attempt to control, manipulate or force. You also become aware of the difference between working hard vs. smart, providing more ease and how simple life can be and human control based on fears, clarity. Spiritual living with a connection to GOD, shows us insecurities, negativity, judgment, and limitations makes it more difficult. Human control comes from a limited thinking perspective, since the mind uses only about 13% and spirit being living as a human connected to GOD has unlimited intelligence and pure love. With human control there is a tendency to come from 'I know it all' mentality.

The inner Spirit and GOD-Universe connection comes from the awareness, 'the more I know, the less I really know since the humaness is always evolving.' From this place of unknown we learn unlimited potential and the mind chatter relaxes. You're able to listen as a spirit being connected to GOD-Universe for guidance. Sometimes the waiting is the hardest part, which requires patience and being present in the moment. If you are use to being a *doer first and being comes second,* the human will want to kick in and start to take action. This action can be premature and cause unnecessary struggles. As you learn to let go of human control, you experience fewer frustrations and greater acceptance. You realize that frustrations only feed the human control to want to push harder and work harder. Whereas, spirit being living as a human being usually says it's based on universal timing and patience is in order. Trust and faith is the best medicine knowing you're doing the best you can bringing out the greatness in you.

Each and every day if you master going within and being silent, you'll discover great treasures. As you live in the moment with appreciation and gratitude, you see and experience heighten beauty and pureness of love. From this place, you become aware of any limiting or out dated beliefs that are holding you back from acquiring any intention that's in alignment with GOD's purpose for you. It becomes easier to transform them peacefully. When you get out of your own way and become your own best friend, it's so much easier to manifest things in life. The bigger the desire, the stronger the hold is on the desired intention. The greater the attachment to the desire, the more the human wants to get involved, creating more difficulties. Surrendering, releases the ego from attempting to control or force the desire to manifest, lessening the emotional attachment. This makes it with greater ease and joy. By observing subjectively what we're holding on to, in the form of attachment, the greater the awareness and the easier it is to let it go. Those that live in a fear-driven mentality will experience more hardships if they let it run their life. Making excuses for those hardships, such as the desired goals that have not materialized and the unjust and unfavorable situations, is not going to improve the situation. It will only add frustrations. And playing the victim role by moaning and groaning when life seems to bring one problem after another will not make the problems go away. It will only add more problems. Sitting in the pity-pot won't clean it up. It will only stink up the environment, leading to a victim mentality making life more miserable.

The real courage comes by moving into a student role and take effective steps within. Taking responsibility for what was created in one's life as an adult and know each of us is responsible for transforming and bettering our life. Even if you may have been a victim as a child, as an adult you can choose differently. Sometimes it is necessary to examining the mind programs within and finding the 'weeds' in your life. This is demonstrated hearing 'broken records,' the same repeated stories being played over and over again that are not serving your well-being. Look for those destructive seeds that were planted and that you kept feeding. If there are any excuses as to why these seeds happened and how they affected your well-being, agree to STOP discussing them. If you find yourself blaming others for why you don't have the life you want, agree to stop finding fault for what is not happening in your life then you are ready to take a positive approach to life.

Our mind is like a computer, in that what we store in our minds we 'print' out verbally. The more we repeat the same thoughts, the greater the belief will become and the results in your life are a reflection of these thoughts. By choosing to observe the mind chatter and investigating the pattern behind it, you're better equipped to break the pattern of the dysfunctional habit. You'll move into clarity and greater understanding eventually with commitment, focus, persistence, patience, trust, allowing, acceptance, attentive listening to GOD-Universe guidance and a Serendipity focus. As you focus on self-care and self-love, it becomes easier to relax and go with the flow. Affirmation is an amazing tool to shift the thought patterns to ones that demonstrate positive, loving behaviors. Destructive thoughts are like weeds that kill us inside and stop us from living life fully and appreciating what life has to offer. Fertilizing our minds with loving, kind and affirming thoughts helps create a more empowering rich and fulfilling lifestyle. Relationships with others, is another way to explore your thought programs and refine areas in your life to live as a spirit being having a human experience and connected to GOD-Universe. When we come from an emotional charge, this is the first step to looking within to see what the other person is showing you directly or indirectly from their behavior. The emotional charge is a form of judgment and when you look at it from a response of love rather than react from human personalization, you receive greater clarity.

Earth is a form of school that teaches us to have a healthier self-image and greater inner strength, thereby having healthier relationships with others. By learning to depersonalize the human self-absorption in relationships you gather answers more peaccfully. Personalization comes from a victim place, feeling someone is doing something 'to you.' You're better equipped to respond in love with yourself and in relationships when you depersonalize the human self-absorbed focus during an emotionally charged situation. Depersonalizing helps you move away from self-absorption and more into acceptance and greater understanding. When you respond from a place of love you can learn, grow and understand what steps to take. As you choose to live a more peace-focused lifestyle, you come more fully into living life on purpose. As you live more on purpose, your relationships are more easeful. Living life with purpose is living fully from a genuine place of love. This exemplifies forgiveness, sharing, nurturing, acceptance and compassion. For you to truly live on purpose, it's necessary to *BE* love, sharing love unconditionally and standing strong in truth in spite of any unjustness and unfairness. It is not about the unjustness and unfairness and giving your power to that level of belief and allowing your truth to become that illusion. If you give your power to that level of belief or blame others for their unjust or unfair behaviors, you start to behave from a place of pain, anger and hatred. I love when Mother Mary said, "invite me when you have a peace rally," after being invited to an anti-war rally.

Living on purpose means forgiveness to those who are not as aware or awakened to divine love. To have compassion for those who forget or behave in unloving ways. To understand that they're making mistakes and sometimes don't understand or know any better, so you bless them and decide through discernment what is best for the well being of both. Giving your power away to those who behave in unjust or unfair manners only contributes to talking 'at' each other, to fighting and to more pain. It is a waste of energy. You're not responsible for others' actions. You're only responsible for your own. To stand tall and courageous in the universal laws of integrity and live on *Purpose* is being a self-directed leader that is living fully with purpose. As you choose to live more fully with purpose, you respond in love and stand strong in truth. Standing in truth will remind those that forgot or are not fully awakened to wake up to love. It may not happen at that moment, yet in GOD-Universal time it WILL happen.

Peaceful relationships will begin to take place as we take the time to attentively listen and accept each other. Love comes from taking the time to truly care and share. When we all can truly come from a place of being fully conscious in the moment and take the time to accept each other, we will live in a more peaceful world. *Judgment and wars comes from bias thoughts, preconceived notions and lack of acceptance. Divine love, a spirit being connected to GOD-Universe is portrayed as one who chooses to stay present, using active listening, sharing from unconditional love, and accepting others.* In all the religions, countries and each other learning to come from a place of genuine interest and acceptance for our differences is coming from a place of divinity in love.

A peaceful world begins when we truly can forgive our past and achieve greater wisdom from the lessons behind these experiences. When we *choose* to care and make the world a better place knowing we are all one in spirit having a human experience and connected to GOD from that place. It starts with each of us and really begins with all of us. *Do we have to go through war-struggle before we choose peace? Please choose to make a difference through peace, unconditional love, and enjoying life.* God Bless you all.

LIFE IS A MYSTERY

Life is a wonder, sometimes as loud as thunder
Life is a mystery, leaving one with a history

Sharers are true believers, continuing on their path to truth, to laugh & share, attracting those who care

A Bad Attitude, A Good Attitude

Quit—Carry a heavy thing called a bad attitude.
Continue—Carry a mind of peace and a positive attitude.

Quit—Think—can't.
Continue—Think—can.

Quit—Judge and criticize others on areas of one's fear.
Continue—Accept and take responsibility for your own fear.

Quit—Look at good days as luck and bad days with blame.
Continue—Look at all days with joy and appreciation; going with the flow and enjoying the simple things in life.

Quit—Push and pull, control and fight
Continue—Share, accept and love

Quit—Life as a destination
Continue—Life as a process

What one believes, one will perceive, and eventually receive-true manifestation. It takes far less energy to have a positive attitude than a non-positive attitude.

- Angelica Rose

ANGELICA ROSE
THE HEART OF MOTIVATION

Angelica Rose, An Angel Walk-in, is an Angel Messenger, Inner Spirit Activation Specialist since 1991, International Radio Host, Certified Hypnotist, Writer, Minister of LOVE, and Author of EBooks, Relaxation CDs, MP3s, MP4s, Talk on Spiritual Oneness and Inspirational Stickers. Angelica also created Online Spiritual Journey series on MP3 and MP4.

Angelica's mission is to operate from the Angelic Plane on this planet committed to ANGELIC LOVE FREQUENCY. Angel assists those who have a loving heart and are choosing to Live a life of prosperity, peace, joy, love, and vitality and would like the assistance of the pure love energies beings I channel. Angelica operates on the Angelic Plane where she relates to Pure Love Energy.

As an Angel Walk-In, She provides Angel Messages without human filters., Inner Spirit Activation Sessions, Energy Alignments, Monthly Channeled Events, Meditation Classes, Hypnosis Sessions, Public Classes and Speaking Engagements that enhance your spiritual path providing for deeper awareness, greater clarity, and heightened levels of love, joy, peace, vitality, and prosperity. She does this with the help of Ascended Starseed Beings, Angelic Realm and the Ascended Masters where she becomes a conduit for their pure loving energies as well as channels messages.

Media Expertise:
Angelica also has media expertise in a variety of areas such as, broadcasting an educational radio show on KEZX, producing, "The Entrepreneurial Television Show," publishing educational articles in a variety of national publications, being a guest on KIRO television, "Merissa at 9," and numerous talk radio shows, and being interviewed on a variety of national magazines. She broadcasts I love Angels on Blogtalk Radio.

https://angelroselove.wixsite.com/love